Epworth Epworth League

The International Convention of the Epworth League

Epworth Epworth League

The International Convention of the Epworth League

ISBN/EAN: 9783743336209

Manufactured in Europe, USA, Canada, Australia, Japa

Cover: Foto ©ninafisch / pixelio.de

Manufactured and distributed by brebook publishing software (www.brebook.com)

Epworth Epworth League

The International Convention of the Epworth League

Souvenir Programme

3rd International Convention

OF THE

EPWORTH LEAGUE

HELD IN

Toronto, Canada

JULY 15th, 16th, 17th and 18th, 1897.

TORONTO:
METHODIST BOOK AND PUBLISHING HOUSE
33 RICHMOND ST. W.

"I desire to form a League, offensive and defensive, with every soldier of Jesus Christ."—*John Wesley.*

MOTTOES.

"**Look Up, Lift Up**"—Methodist Episcopal Church, and Methodist Church, Canada.

"**All for Christ**"—Methodist Episcopal Church South.

"**One Heart, One Way**"—Wesley Guild, England.

BX
8205
A54
1897

"We live to make our Church a power in the land, while we live to love every other Church that exalts our Christ."—*Bishop Simpson.*

TORONTO

THE QUEEN CITY OF CANADA

"I dreamed not then that, ere the rolling year
Had filled its circle, I should wander here
In musing awe; should tread this wondrous world,
See all its store of inland waters hurled
In one vast volume down Niagara's steep
Or calm behold them in transparent sleep,
Where the blue hills of old Toronto shed
Their evening shadows o'er Ontario's bed."

—MOORE.

TORONTO is known as the "Queen City of Canada," and certainly the title is not a misnomer. Montreal is recognized as the commercial metropolis of the Dominion, Ottawa is the political centre, Hamilton is noted for its manufacturing interests, but Toronto is the undoubted educational, social and religious centre, and everything considered, exceeds in interest any of its sister cities. Those who wish to see a typical Canadian city cannot do better than visit Toronto.

The Queen City is located on Lake Ontario, about two hours' sail from Niagara, and a little more than 200 miles from Detroit. It is the capital of the Province of Ontario, and has tributary to it as fine an agricultural country as the sun shines on. Viewed from the water the city is not seen at its best. The land on which it is built rises considerably to the north, but not sufficiently to make an imposing appearance from the deck of the incoming steamer. The visitor will find it, however, a most charming place with many points of interest. It has a population of about 200,000 people, as industrious, as upright, and as happy as any in the world.

CANTILEVER BRIDGE OVER NIAGARA RIVER.

TORONTO AS A SUMMER RESORT.

Dr. E. Herbert Adams, of Toronto, who has given much attention to the subject, says:

There are few cities in the world that are more admirably situated or more naturally adapted for an all-round summer resort than Toronto, the Queen City of the Lakes.

Situated as it is, in the heart of the temperate zone, its climate tempered and made equable by the broad waters of Lake Ontario, with a beautiful harbor which renders boating and bathing safe and pleasant pastimes during the summer months, together with many other advantages, Ontario's capital can hold her own against the world as an ideal summer resort.

VIEW IN MOUNT PLEASANT CEMETERY.

By wintering in Florida, California, Italy or the French Riviera, and summering in Toronto, or the vicinity, an equable all the year round temperature can be obtained; for Toronto in summer possesses a very similar climate to that which is found in the balmy south during its fashionable season, when Northerners doff their furs and leave their land of ice and snow for the everglades and flowering shrubs and zephyrs of the Sunny South. And the pleasures and novelties in which the denizens of the north revel during their southern trip are but similar to those in which their heat-stricken confreres of the south may indulge during the summer, should they come north to the many and excellent summer resorts of Ontario, of which Toronto, the distributing centre, is by no means the least attractive or healthful.

There is endless variety to be found amidst the pleasures of the summer resorts of Toronto and neighborhood. Here are gaiety and fashion, solitude or roughing it, modern civilization and primeval forest, cascade and river, lakes of all sizes from the immensity of the Great Lakes to the placid waters of the miniature lily ponds of Muskoka. Here you can paddle your own canoe on the lagoons of Toronto Island, spread your white canvas to the breeze on Toronto Bay, or, boarding one of the majestic

DRIVE IN HIGH PARK.

ironclad steamers of the Niagara Line, after a few hours' pleasant sail on the lake and a brief trip on the electric railway the roar of Niagara greets your ears. To the north are the Georgian Bay, with its 30,000 islands and deep woods, and the delightful Muskoka Lakes with their stupendous rocks, their health-giving pines, the softest of water for bathing and as good fishing and hunting as can be found on the continent. To the east are Balmy Beach, Scarboro' Heights, Victoria Park, Lake Scugog with its fine maskinonge fishing and the beautiful Peterborough chain of lakes, the delight of the canoeist and the fisherman; while farther on is the enchanting region of the Thousand Islands and the Rapids of the St.

Lawrence. To the west are High Park, the beautiful Humber River, Mimico, Long Branch, Lorne Park, Oakville, Burlington Beach, and Hamilton; while to the south is Toronto Island, and across the lake are Port Dalhousie, St. Catharines, and Grimsby Park. Indeed, there is no other city in America which has a larger or better equipped fleet of palatial passenger steamers and ferries plying to resorts within easy reach, and where daily trips can be had at so small a cost.

TORONTO STREET, SHOWING POST OFFICE AT HEAD.

CLIMATE OF TORONTO.

In regard to the climate Dr. Adams says:

The summer climate of Toronto is remarkably healthful and equable, and is one of the finest in the world. The days are bright and sunny; there are no mosquitos or sand flies, and no diseases due to climatic influences, such as malaria or hay fever. Sunstroke is almost unknown in the region.

During the summer months the mercury seldom rises above 80 degrees or falls below 55, while the average is 66.25 degrees. July is generally the hottest month. The rainfall in summer is not excessive, an occasional thunderstorm only serving to cool the atmosphere and refresh the foliage. The average summer humidity is about 71 degrees, which is equal, and indeed superior in many cases, to many of the best resorts of Florida, California and the Carolinas.

The streets being well shaded by luxuriant and ornamental shade trees, it is not a hot city at any time, while the roads being clean and well paved and sprinkled by civic watering-carts, there are no great clouds of dust as in many resorts. There are no cyclones, hurricanes or very high winds. Almost every plant that requires a hot summer can thrive in Toronto. The proximity of such a large body of fresh water as that of Lake Ontario undoubtedly assists largely in equalizing the temperature. The climatic conditions of Toronto, such as humidity, temperature and number of clear, sunny days, compare favorably in summer with those of the most noted resorts of the world. The average temperature in summer is between ten and twenty degrees hotter than that of the resorts of Georgia, Florida and South Carolina in winter, and between ten and twenty degrees cooler than the temperature of these States in summer, while the elevation above the sea is about the same, and there is little difference in humidity.

The following table shows the maximum, minimum and mean temperature during the summer months of Toronto, Atlantic City and Denver:

TORONTO—Average of 51 years.

	MEAN.	MAX.	MIN.
June	62.05	74.57	54.26
July	67.67	73.56	54.70
August	66.25	75.02	57.11

ATLANTIC CITY, N.J.

	MEAN.	MAX.	MIN.
June	60.0	72.6	59.5
July	68.8	73.5	64.1
August	72.0	76.8	67.1

DENVER, COL.

	MEAN.	MAX.	MIN.
June	63.4	75.7	51.4
July	68.9	81.3	56.5
August	69.2	83.0	55.5

From these tables it will be seen that Toronto is not quite so hot as Atlantic City, N.J., and that the mean daily temperature is very near that of Denver, save that there is a greater daily variation in the latter city.

Owing to the evenness and salubrity of its climate, together with the efficiency of the civic sanitary system, Toronto is a remarkably healthy city. It is admirably situated from a sanitary standpoint, the land sloping gently downward to the lake, thus affording a natural downfall for the sewage.

THE STREETS OF TORONTO.

Toronto has 250 miles of streets, the majority of them well paved with asphalt, brick, and wood, and kept quite clean. The main business thoroughfares are King, Yonge, and Queen streets. King Street marks the boundary line between the wholesale and retail districts, and is lined by many magnificent mercantile institutions. Yonge Street begins at

KING STREET, LOOKING WEST.

Toronto Bay and runs directly north, dividing the city into two almost equal halves. It continues in almost a direct line through the country to Lake Simcoe, and is said to be, with the exception of the old Roman roads in England, the longest street in the world. Queen Street is remarkable for the number of its retail stores, second-hand shops, etc. It has nearly five miles of shop front, and over fifteen hundred stores. University Avenue, on which the Headquarters Building is located, is a wide street, with six rows of luxuriant shade trees and two drive-ways.

SHERBOURNE STREET.

THE PARKS.

The park area of the city is 1,153 acres, and these resting places are scattered in all sections. Perhaps the most attractive is known as "The Island," which contains 325 acres, and is situated about a mile and a half from the southern limit of the city across a beautiful bay, on which large and commodious ferries run back and forth every fifteen minutes. Dr. Adams thus describes the Island :

"The Island, as it is popularly called, has done much toward making Toronto the attractive Summer Resort which it is, and has also contributed largely to the healthfulness and prosperity of its citizens. The formation of the Island is itself somewhat extraordinary, consisting as it does of a sandy strip of land about six miles in length, narrow in places, and widening out at its western extremity to its greatest breadth, which is here about a mile. Originally it formed a peninsula, what is now the eastern channel being continuous with the mainland. Its widest part is curiously intersected with miniature ponds and lagoons, in which are to be found beautiful bulrushes, white and yellow water lilies and aquatic plants, and which once were the continual abiding-place of turtles, frogs and innumerable water fowl. These lagoons now are the delight of the canoeist and boatman, and are safe and pleasant places for indulgence in aquatic sports of all kinds. The appearance of the Island is very singular. It lies so low that Ontario's broad expanse can be seen over it.

"Centre Island is now covered with numerous trees, and an even and well-carpeted lawn, which form a handsome park, and it is a great family resort. On some portions of the Island there is but a single tree, which adds to the peculiarity of its appearance. Pretty villas, summer cottages and hotels are scattered over its surface. At Centre Island the Royal Canadian Yacht Club have a handsome club house.

QUEEN'S PARK.

"Hanlan's Point, at the western extremity, is the Coney Island of Toronto. Here of an afternoon or evening a fine band discourses sweet music. Here are the hurdy-gurdy, the merry-go-round, etc. The promenades are usually thronged with people, some in ordinary summer attire, others in boating jerseys and camping costume or tennis suits. Most have come across from the city on the ferries; others, with their sweethearts or friends, have crossed the bay in canoe, rowboat or yacht, while others who reside in cottages or tents on the Island have strolled to the Point to join the merry and motley throng.

"At the centre of the Island, or Island Park, as it is called, the scene is far different. It is more of a family resort where children can romp and play with safety; a breathing spot and place of rest and quiet for the busy business man and the tired mother, and is patronized largely by people of quieter tastes than the frequenters of Hanlan's Point. The breakwater, which protects a large portion of the shore of the Island, is a favorite promenade of a summer afternoon or evening. Here you will see typical specimens of Canadian people, venerable old age, middle life with its sturdy manhood and womanhood, athletic young men and beautiful maidens in all the buoyancy of life, and childhood with the flush of innocence on the cheek. The low and shelving sandy beach of the lake shore affords safe

HORTICULTURAL GARDENS.

and excellent facilities for bathing. Wiman's baths at the eastern extremity of the Island, and the baths at Hanlan's Point at the western extremity, are the chief bathing centres, and are largely patronized by young and old. Bathing suits and dressing rooms may here be obtained at small cost. The Amateur Aquatic Association of the Island contributes considerably to the spiciness of life on the Island. The aquatic sporting events provided under their auspices are much appreciated by the crowds who gather to witness them. They consist of paddling, sculling and swimming races, canoe upsets, hurry-scurries, diving contests, tub races and various other forms of aquatic amusements."

VIEW AT ISLAND PARK.

Another park worthy of mention is High Park, a beautiful stretch of undulating country of 375 acres, containing ponds, ravines, breezy hills and beautiful picnic spots. At the extreme north of the city is Reservoir Park, one of the most charming little places upon the continent. Here is a reservoir capable of containing about 45,000,000 gallons of water, surrounded by forty-two acres of park land, kept in magnificent condition. The Horticultural Gardens, a park of ten and a half acres, is a show spot nearly in the centre of the city. It contains a beautiful palm house, with a choice selection of palms, orchids and flowering plants, in addition to handsome grounds laid out with brilliant-colored seasonable flowers. The Pavilion, in which some of the large Convention meetings will be held, is located in the Gardens. Seats are provided through the grounds, which will be found to be a quiet and delightful place in which to rest. Riverside

PARLIAMENT BUILDINGS.

Park, on the banks of the Don, is a very pretty little place. Mount Pleasant Cemetery is a charming spot about three miles from Massey Hall. There are other parks that will repay a visit by those who come to the Convention.

PUBLIC BUILDINGS.

There are a number of splendid public buildings in Toronto. The new City Hall is, with possibly the one in Philadelphia excepted, the largest and finest municipal building in America. Its cost will not be far short of $2,000,000. It is to be regretted that it was not completed in time for the Convention.

NEW CITY HALL.

The Parliament Building has a fine site in the Queen's Park. This edifice cost a million and a half, and, wonderful to relate, was erected for almost exactly the amount estimated before it was commenced. A splendid view of the city can be obtained from the tower.

An English journalist who recently visited the city pays the following tribute to the Legislative Building :

"The new Parliament Building is a superb edifice in brown stone, and in what is known as 'Neo-Grecian' style, and altogether different from any other public building in Canada. The total cost was barely a million and a half dollars, yet the effect, both within and without, is infinitely more impressive and sumptuous than the Capitol at Albany, which cost upwards of $20,000,000. The frescoes and decorations of the interior, particularly that of the legislative chamber, which is fitted up for ninety-four members,

are worth travelling a long way to see. There has been no 'jobbing' here. The oak carving on every hand is really of oak, and not of papier-mache, and the furniture and appointments, even down to the dinner service of the Speaker - which the chief messenger exhibited to me with a proper pride— are of the most solid and sterling description, selected with an eye both to beauty and durability."

Toronto is particularly proud of her Educational Institutions which are clustered around Toronto University in the Queen's Park. The University is a magnificent stone building with quite extensive grounds, which are used by the students for playing football, baseball and lacrosse.

Victoria University is an institution in which Toronto Methodism takes great pride. It is one of the oldest educational establishments in the

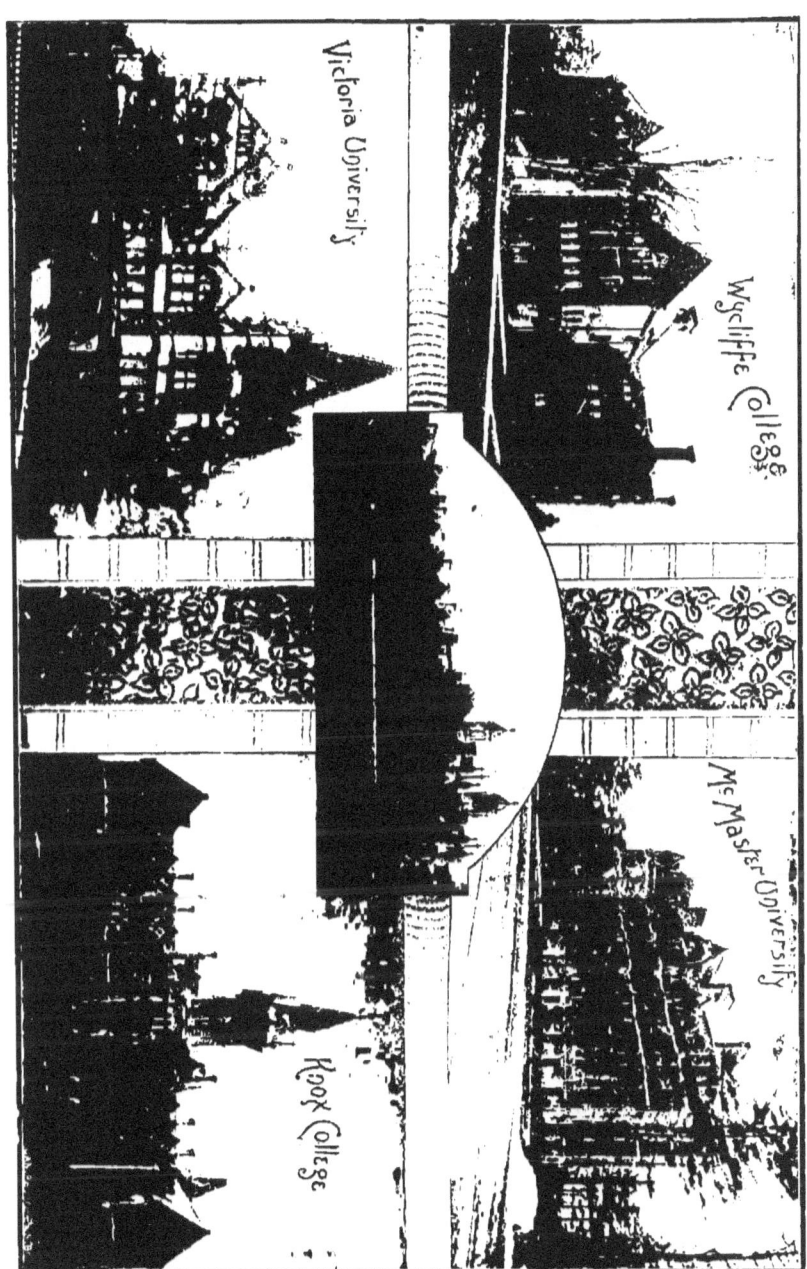

TORONTO COLLEGES.

Dominion, having been founded at Cobourg in the year 1830 under the title of Upper Canada Academy. About five years ago it was removed to Toronto and affiliated with Toronto University. Largely through the munificent gifts of Senator George A. Cox, Hon. John Macdonald, Mr. William Gooderham and Mr. H. A. Massey, a splendid building has been erected in Queen's Park, entirely free of debt. In addition to his subscrip-

UPPER CANADA COLLEGE.

tion of $40,000 during his lifetime, Mr. Massey left the sum of $200,000 to Victoria to be added to its endowment fund. Mr. Massey's generosity also extended to several Methodist colleges outside of the city. Victoria University is one of the handsomest structures in the city, and should be seen by every delegate to the Convention.

NORMAL SCHOOL BUILDING.

There are over fifty Public Schools in Toronto, not including a large number of Separate Schools. There are also three Collegiate Institutes and more than forty Kindergartens. The Public School system of Toronto has no superior anywhere. Education is compulsory for all, and as text-books are free the poorest children can attend.

Osgoode Hall is the seat of the law courts. It is said to be by art critics one of the finest specimens of Grecian architecture on the continent.

In hospitals, asylums and benevolent institutions of various kinds, the city is well equipped, the citizens having provided generously for those upon whom the hand of misfortune has fallen.

OSGOODE HALL.

The Educational Department occupies a whole square in the centre of the city, and comprises some interesting exhibits which are always open to the public free of charge.

The Normal School building has a museum which is worth visiting.

There are three Medical Colleges—Toronto University Medical College, Trinity Medical College, and the Women's Medical College. They are all well conducted and scientifically equipped.

A CITY OF HOMES.

"Except on the main business thoroughfares most of the streets have boulevards of well-kept lawns and shade trees. Many of the residential districts present on each side of the avenue a regular forest line of chestnuts, elms and maples. The residential portion of the city is to the stranger one of the most pleasing features of the town, for Toronto is a veritable 'City of Homes,' and its citizens vie with one another in the artistic appearance and conveniences of their home life. There are no flats as in New York and some other cities, and almost every head of a family, no matter how poor, has a house to himself which he rents or owns. Perhaps nowhere else will be found more unique and artistic architectural designs for private residences than along some of the fashionable residential thoroughfares of Toronto. Delightful glimpses of lawn, flowers and shrubbery are exceedingly common around the homes of the better classes, and even the poorer people often boast their little strip of lawn or modest flower garden. Among the more fashionable residential streets may be mentioned Jarvis, St. George, Sherbourne and Bloor."

THE STREET CARS.

The city possesses a street car system unexcelled on the continent. Rapid transit at cheap fares, in the most comfortable cars that can be devised, are the leading features of its service. For a four-cent fare one can ride upon this system a distance of ten miles from the extreme east end to the extreme west end of the city. By this means tourists are enabled to visit all the points of interest within the municipality at the cheapest rate and the least possible expenditure of time.

The rates of fare, with free transfers to or from any part of city, are: Cash, 5 cents ; night (after 12 p.m.), 10 cents ; tickets, 6 for 25 cents, or 25 for $1.00. Limited tickets, good from 5.30 to 8 a.m., and from 5 to 6.30 in the evening, 8 for 25 cents.

INDEX TO CAR ROUTES.

A.—Yonge Street	. One Blue Light.
B.—Belt Line	. One Red Light.
C.—Bloor and McCaul .	Yellow and White Lights.
D.—Church Street . .	. . Two Red Lights.
E.—Avenue Road . .	. Two White Lights.
F.—Dovercourt Road .	. Two White Lights.
G.—King {Balsam Ave. .	. Two White Lights.
{Kingston Road	. One White Light.
H.—Queen Street West .	. One Green Light.
I.—Dundas Street . .	. Two Green Lights.
J.—College and Yonge .	Blue and Yellow Lights.
K.—Bathurst Street .	. Red and White Lights.
L.—Winchester Street .	. Blue and Red Lights.
M.—Parliament Street .	White and Yellow Lights.
N.—Carlton and College .	. . One Yellow Light.
O.—Broadview Ave. .	. Red and Green Lights.

VIEW AT ROSEDALE.

TORONTO GENERAL HOSPITAL.

HOW TO SEE THE CITY.

Many pleasant trips can be made by street car, a few of which are suggested:

1. Take the Belt Line, which runs on King, Sherbourne, Bloor Streets and Spadina Avenue, making a complete circle. For one fare passengers can ride seven miles and get off at the very place from whence they started. This run will enable visitors to view three fine residence streets, and one of the principal business streets. Along the way may be seen St. James' Cathedral, Horticultural Gardens, Sherbourne Street, Central, and Broadway Tabernacle Methodist Churches, St. Andrew's Presbyterian Church, McMaster University, and other interesting places.

2. To reach High Park, take either King or Queen Street cars west to the end of the line, then walk a few steps to the entrance of Park. If desired, return journey can be made by College and Yonge cars, leaving the Park at the north-east gate.

3. Queen's Park is nearly in the centre of the city. Take College and Yonge or Carlton and College Street cars, and ask to be put off at the Parliament Buildings. A walk straight up University Avenue will lead to the Parliament Buildings. The Park is in the rear.

4. For Toronto Island, ferry boats leave wharf at foot of Yonge Street every fifteen minutes. A fine trip is to take boat to Island Park and walk around the lake shore to Hanlan's Point (about two miles), and take boat from there to the city. If there is not time for this, and a choice has to be

UNION DEPOT.

made between Island Park and Hanlan's Point, the former place should be visited. Delegates are requested to purchase Island Ferry tickets at Ticket Office at Convention Headquarters.

5. Reservoir Park can be reached by Yonge Street cars north. It will be necessary to walk a short distance after leaving the cars; but it is a very pretty spot worth visiting.

6. Mount Pleasant Cemetery is a couple of miles from the city, on Yonge Street north. After leaving Yonge Street cars take Metropolitan Railway, which passes the Cemetery gates.

7. Long Branch and Lorne Park are beautiful summer resorts a few miles west of Toronto. Steamboats run from foot of Yonge Street at regular intervals.

CAB TARIFF.

For points that cannot be conveniently reached by street cars, cabs can be secured at very moderate prices. The following is the cab tariff, and no driver has the right to charge more than the figures named:

RATES OF FARES AUTHORIZED BY CITY ORDINANCES RELATIVE TO PUBLIC CARRIAGES. ETC., ETC.

Every cabman on each occasion when his cab is hired, when demanded, shall hand his card to the person employing him. No fare is to be paid to any cabman who refuses to hand his card to the person employing him, or who demands a greater rate than allowed by the following tariff:

THE CAB LIMITS.

No. 1 Division will be composed of that portion of the city lying between Bathurst Street, both sides; Bloor Street, both sides; Sumach Street, both sides, and the Bay.

No. 2 Division.—Dufferin Street, both sides; northern city limits, Pape Avenue and the Bay.

No. 3 Division.—Western city limits, northern city limits, eastern city limits and the Bay.

ONE OR TWO-HORSE CABS.

First Division—One or two persons, 50 cents; each additional person, 25 cents. Second Division—One or two persons, 75 cents; each additional person, 25 cents. Third Division—One or two persons, $1.00; each additional person, 25 cents. The fare by the hour for one or four persons in a two-horse cab is $1.00, each additional person, 25 cents. The fare by the hour for one or three persons in a single-horse cab is 75 cents, and for each subsequent hour, 60 cents.

NIGHT TARIFF.

The charge for cabs after 12 o'clock midnight to 6 a.m. shall be one-half more than the aforesaid tariff.

CHILDREN.

No fare shall be charged for children under eight years of age in charge of an adult. Children over eight years and under twelve years charged half fare; over that age, full fare.

BAGGAGE.

One trunk and articles that may be placed inside the cab are to be carried free. For every other article placed on the outside of the cab the cabman is entitled to five cents.

SCENE ON TORONTO BAY.

FOR BICYCLISTS.

No doubt many delegates will bring their bicycles with them. They will find a number of very good streets for enjoying the exhilarating pastime of wheeling.

One pleasant run is to start from the Armory and wheel up University Avenue to the Parliament Buildings, turning to the left and coming out on St. George Street; go to head of St. George Street and back to starting point.

Another would be up Jarvis Street, east to Sherbourne, and down Sherbourne to Queen and west to starting point.

One of the most popular "spins" is to take College Street west into High Park, returning the same way or by way of King or Queen.

There is a cinder path for about four miles along the Lake Shore at western terminus of Queen Street.

CYCLING IN HIGH PARK.

Bicyclists in High Park should beware of coasting or even riding down the hills. They are tempting, but dangerous, and those who wish to preserve life and limb will do well to walk down.

Arrangements have been completed to hold Sunrise Prayer Meetings for bicyclists on Friday and Saturday mornings. An early run will be made, starting from Headquarters Building at 5.30 a.m. The prayer meeting will be held at some point a few miles away, probably in High Park on Friday morning, and Reservoir Park on Saturday.

Those who bring bicycles across the line will have to put up a deposit with the customs officers, which will be refunded on return. This will not apply to those who are members of the A. W. A., as their badge of membership will be accepted in lieu of deposit.

Wheels can be hired in Toronto at two hours for 25 cents in the day time and 35 cents in the evenings.

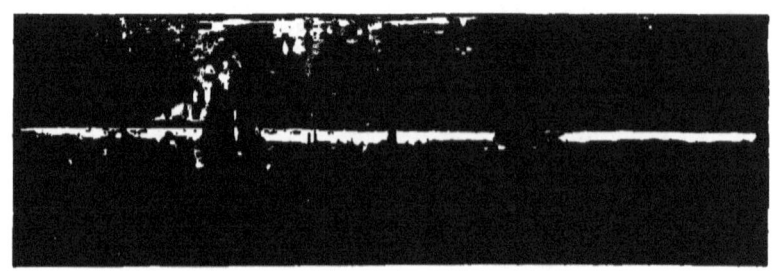

PLACES OF INTEREST IN TORONTO.

Lieutenant-Governor's Residence, King and Simcoe streets.
Parliament Buildings, Queen's Park.
Custom House, Cor. Yonge and Front streets.
Provincial Lunatic Asylum, Queen Street West.
Canada Life Buildings, King Street West.
Exhibition Grounds and Crystal Palace, Dufferin Street.
Osgoode Hall, Queen Street West.
Queen's Park, head of College Avenue.
Monument to the Heroes of Ridgeway, Queen's Park.
Monument to Hon. Geo. Brown, Queen's Park.
Meteorological Observatory, Queen's Park.
School of Practical Science, Queen's Park.
Young Women's Christian Association, Elm Street.
University Buildings, Queen's Park.
Horticultural Gardens, Gerrard and Sherbourne streets.
Normal School, Museum, etc., Gould Street.
Y. M. C. A. Rooms, Yonge and McGill streets.
Mount Pleasant Cemetery, Deer Park.
St. James' Cemetery, Parliament and Wellesley streets.
Post Office, Adelaide Street East.
Confederation Life Buildings, Yonge and Richmond streets.
Central Prison, Strachan Avenue.
Knox College, Spadina Avenue.
McMaster University, Bloor Street West.
Trinity College, Queen Street West.
Victoria University, Queen's Park.
Ontario Society of Artists, King Street West.
Upper Canada College, head of Avenue Road.
Canadian Institute, Museum and Library, Richmond Street East.

SIDE TRIPS FROM TORONTO.

For those who can spend a week or two, there are any number of charming summer resorts within easy reach of Toronto. The Muskoka District is perhaps the most famous summering place in Canada.

This is a section of country that Nature apparently designed for a summer resort, and no mistake was made in its preparation. For about fifty square miles the country is a succession of lakes, rivers and rocky

SHADOW RIVER, MUSKOKA.

islets of the most delightful description. The water is noted for its tonic qualities, due to an entire absence of lime; and the air of these high lands is most salubrious. There are any number of summer hotels on Lake Muskoka and adjoining water stretches, where excellent accommodation can be obtained from $1.00 to $2.00 a day.

Those who desire further information regarding points of interest outside of Toronto should consult the "Canadian Summer Resort Guide," which will be on sale at the Headquarters Building.

RETURNING FROM DEER HUNT, MUSKOKA.

ONTARIO LADIES' COLLEGE, WHITBY, ONTARIO.

ONTARIO LADIES' COLLEGE.

One place in the vicinity of Toronto that may be especially mentioned is the Ontario Ladies' College, located at Whitby, about thirty miles east of the city. All Epworth Leaguers and their friends are cordially invited to visit this institution and see for themselves what Canadian Methodism is doing for the higher education of young women. Visitors from the United States will be made specially welcome.

The buildings are modelled after one of the old palatial homes of English aristocracy, and are unique in internal decoration and external appearance. Every modern comfort in the shape of steam heating, electric lighting, and the best sanitary plumbing is provided. The course of study embraces a Preparatory Course leading to the various teachers' certificates and University Matriculation, also a regular University Course with honors, extending through the Freshman and Sophomore Years of Toronto University.

The Conservatory of Music in connection with the College affords the best facilities for the study of piano, pipe organ, violin, guitar, vocal music and harmony. The fine art, elocution, commercial and domestic economy departments are under the direction of gifted specialists.

NOTE THE RATES—Board, laundry, lights and tuition in English branches for one year, $150. Instrumental music and an hour's practice daily, $36 additional.

The Principal, Rev. J. J. Hare, Ph.D., Whitby, Ont., will be pleased to forward Calendar giving full information about the College to any who may send for it.

VICTORIA PARK, TORONTO.

BITS IN MUSKOKA.

THIRD INTERNATIONAL

Epworth League Convention,

TORONTO, CANADA.

July 15th to 18th, 1897.

PARTICIPATED IN BY THE

Methodist Episcopal Church, Methodist Episcopal Church South,
and Methodist Church, Canada.

THE EPWORTH LEAGUE was organized May 15th, 1889, in the city of Cleveland by the amalgamation of five Methodist Young People's Societies. Since then its growth has been phenomenal. The number of Chapters in the Methodist Episcopal Church alone on the eight anniversaries is as follows :

May 15,	1890	-	-	-	-	1,820 Chapters.
"	1891	-	-	-	-	5,602 "
"	1892	-	-	-	-	8,102 "
"	1893	-	-	-	-	10,200 "
"	1894	-	-	-	-	12,519 "
"	1895	-	-	-	-	14,719 "
"	1896	-	-	-	-	16,302 "
"	1897	-	-	-	-	17,500 "

There are 2,750,000 members in the Methodist Episcopal Church, and already the membership of the Epworth League is 1,600,000.

The number of Chapters in the Methodist Episcopal Church South has increased during the past year from 2,000 to 3,300, and the total membership is about 225,000. The League in Canada numbers about 1,800

Chapters and 80,000 members, so that the total strength of the Epworth League is in the neighborhood of 22,300 Chapters and nearly 2,000,000 members.

INTERNATIONAL GATHERINGS.

First International Convention at Cleveland, O., June 29, 30, July 1st and 2nd, 1893—attended by five thousand persons.

Second, at Chattanooga, Tenn., June 27-30, 1895 — attendance, ten thousand.

Third, at Toronto, Canada, July 15-18—expected attendance, twenty thousand.

Board of Control of the Epworth League, Methodist Episcopal Church.

BISHOP W. X. NINDE, Detroit, Mich.
Rev. W. I. HAVEN, 33 Marion Street, Brookline, Mass.
Rev. J. H. COLEMAN, D.D., Albany, N.Y.
Rev. J. W. E. BOWEN, D.D., South Atlanta, Ga.
Rev. E. M. MILLS, D.D., Elmira, N.Y.
Rev. S. O. ROYAL, D.D., Troy, Ohio.
R. R. DOHERTY, Ph.D., 150 Fifth Avenue, New York City.
W. L. WOODCOCK, Altoona, Pa.
JOHN A. PATTEN, Chattanooga, Tenn.
F. A. CHAMBERLAIN, Security Bank, Minneapolis, Minn.
C. E. PIPER, 1238 Stock Exchange Building, Chicago, Ill.
L. J. NORTON, Napa, Cal.
R. S. COPELAND, M.D., Ann Arbor, Mich.
H. A. SCHROETTER, Covington, Ky.
F. D. FULLER, Topeka, Kan.
CHARLES R. MAGEE, 38 Bromfield Street, Boston, Mass.
Rev. E. S. OSBON, D.D., 178 Wharburton Avenue, Yonkers, N.Y.
Rev. S. A. MORSE, D.D., Corning, N.Y.
F. W. TUNNELL, Germantown, Pa.
B. E. HELMAN, Cleveland, Ohio.
Rev. M. M. ALSTON, Griffin, Ga.
Rev. W. D. PARR, D.D., Kokomo, Ind.
Rev. J. B. ALBROOK, D.D., Marshalltown, Iowa.
Rev. W. H. JORDAN, D.D., Sioux Falls, S.D.
B. L. PAINE, M.D., Lincoln, Neb.
Rev. J. W. VANCLEVE, Mt. Vernon, Ill.
Rev. FRANK GARY, Galveston, Texas. (807 Ave. H.)
Rev. WM. KOENEKE, D.D., Belleville, Ill.
Rev. J. W. BENNETT, Bozeman, Mont.

THE ARMORY, CONVENTION HEADQUARTERS.

General Cabinet, Epworth League.

Rev. Wm. X. Ninde, D.D., LL.D., Detroit, Mich., President.
Rev. W. I. Haven, 33 Marion Street, Brookline, Mass., 1st Vice-President.
Rev. E. M. Mills, D.D., Elmira, N.Y., 2nd Vice-President.
R. R. Doherty, Ph.D., 150 Fifth Avenue, New York City, 3rd Vice-President.
Mr. J. A. Patten, Chattanooga, Tenn., 4th Vice-President.
Rev. Edwin A. Schell, D.D., Chicago, Ill., General Secretary.
Mr. C. E. Piper, 1238 Stock Exchange Building, Chicago, Ill., Treasurer.
Rev. J. F. Berry, D.D., Chicago, Ill., Editor *Epworth Herald.*
Rev. F. L. Nagler, D.D., Cincinnati, Ohio, German Assistant Secretary.

Epworth League Board, Methodist Episcopal Church South.

Bishop R. K. Hargrove, President.
Rev. J. E. Harrison, 1st Vice-President.
Rev. J. W. Newman, 2nd Vice-President.
Professor W. R. Webb, 3rd Vice-President.
J. U. Rust, Treasurer.
Rev. S. A. Steel, D.D., General Secretary.

John B. Rader.	A. E. Whitaker.
J. T. Browninski.	W. B. Thompson.
J. D. Crooks.	J. A. Clifton.
J. E. Wray.	W. W. Pinson.

EXECUTIVE COMMITTEE.

Bishop R. K. Hargrove.	Rev. J. E. Harrison.
Professor W. R. Webb.	J. U. Rust.
Rev. S. A. Steel.	

W. S. Parks, Office Assistant.

Epworth League and Sunday School Board, Methodist Church, Canada.

Rev. A. CARMAN, D.D., General Superintendent, Belleville, Ont., President of Epworth League Board.
Rev. A. C. CREWS, Wesley Buildings, Toronto, Ont., General Secretary.
J. W. FLAVELLE, ESQ., Toronto, Ont., General Treasurer.
WILLIAM JOHNSON, ESQ., Belleville, Ont., 1st Vice-President.
Rev. W. J. FORD, LL.B., Clinton, Ont., 2nd Vice-President.
Rev. R. W. WOODSWORTH, Woodstock, Ont., 3rd Vice-President.
J. S. DEACON, ESQ., Milton, Ont., 4th Vice-President.
Rev. C. W. WATCH, Brighton, Ont., 5th Vice-President.
    Rev. J. E. Lanceley, Brampton, Ont.
     " E. N. Baker, Chatham, Ont.
     " J. B. Saunders, D.D., Ottawa, Ont.
     " John Maclean, Ph.D., Neepawa, Man.
     " Dr. Griffith, Brockville, Ont.
     " G. W. Kerby, B.A., St. Catharines, Ont.
     " S. G. Bland, B.A., Smith's Falls, Ont.
     " R. J. Garbutt, LL.B., Birr, Ont.
     " W. W. Andrews, Ph.D., Sackville, N.B.
     " T. W. Hall, Nanaimo, B.C.
     " D. W. Johnston, Canso, N.S.
     " D. Chapman, Woodstock, N.B.
     " W. W. Swann, Cupids, Nfld.
Col. C. S. Jones, Toronto.
C. P. Holton, Belleville, Ont.
N. W. Rowell, Toronto.
John T. Moore, Toronto.
A. B. Powell, London, Ont.
J. S. Deacon, Milton, Ont.
W. Johnston, Belleville, Ont.
F. Myers, Montreal, Que.
M. H. Fieldhouse, Neepawa, Man.
Dr. F. Woodbury, Dartmouth, N.S.
M. Lamont, Fredericton, N.S.
C. P. Ayr, Newfoundland.
A. W. Martin, Newfoundland.
J. Reid, Nova Scotia.

Pulpit Supply Committee.

Rev. Dr. German, Chairman; Rev. E. E. Scott, Secretary; Revs. Jas. Allen, M.A., R. N. Burns, B.A., and J. F. Ockley.

Local Committee of Arrangements.

The following are the names and addresses of the members of the General Executive Committee having the Convention in charge:

Chairman—J. L. HUGHES, corner York and Richmond streets.
Secretary—Dr. W. EARL WILLMOTT, 37 Shuter Street.
Assistant Secretary—W. B. SHORT, 278 Wellington Street West.
Treasurer—A. E. AMES, 10 King Street West.

CHAIRMEN OF COMMITTEES.

Finance—J. R. L. STARR, 60 Victoria Street.
Reception—Col. C. S. JONES, Parliament Buildings.
Registration—B. N. DAVIS, corner Bay and Richmond streets.
Place of Meeting—Rev. A. C. CREWS, Wesley Buildings.
Homes—D. SCOTT, 70 Henry Street.
Decoration—JAMES HALES, 35 Adelaide Street East.
Music—ALEX. MILLS, 35 Adelaide Street East.
Transportation—CHAS. HUDSON, Union Depot.
Local Transportation—R. H. MCBRIDE, 54 King Street East.
Press—H. C. HOCKEN, 106 Yonge Street.

ADDITIONAL MEMBERS.

J. W. St. John, M.P.P.	Rev. Dr. Withrow.
N. W. Rowell.	Dr. J. J. Maclaren.
Rev. Dr. Potts.	Hon. Geo. A. Cox.
Rev. Dr. Burwash.	C. D. Massey.

INDEX TO ENGRAVING.

1. J. L. Hughes, Chairman.
2. Dr. J. J. Maclaren.
3. Chester D. Massey.
4. Col. C. S. Jones.
5. Rev. Dr. Withrow.
6. H. C. Hocken.
7. Alex. Mills.
8. R. H. McBride.
9. Chas. Hudson.
10. D. Scott.
11. N. W. Rowell.
12. B. N. Davis.
13. A. E. Ames.
14. James Hales.
15. Dr. W. E. Willmott.
16. W. B. Short.
17. J. R. L. Starr.

Committee on Resolutions.

Bishop W. X. Ninde, D.D.
Rev. J. H. Coleman, D.D., Albany, N.Y.
Mr. F. D. Fuller, Topeka, Kan.
Rev. A. Carman, D.D., Toronto, Ont.
Rev. R. N. Burns, B.A., Toronto, Ont.
Mr. C. P. Holton, Belleville, Ont.
Rev. E. B. Chappel, St. Louis, Mo.
Rev. E. H. Rawlings, Richmond, Va.
Mr. John R. Pepper, Memphis, Tenn.

LOCAL COMMITTEE OF ARRANGEMENTS.

THE CONVENTION BUILDINGS.

In no city on the continent is there such a cluster of buildings suitable for convention purposes to be found in so small a radius as in Toronto. Within an area of one-sixth of a mile, in the central portion of the city—convenient to all the leading hotels, railway stations and steamboat landings—there are four magnificent edifices with seating capacity for almost thirteen thousand people. This will enable the delegates to take part in those portions of the programme of special individual interest with the minimum loss of time and a consequent maximum measure of profit.

HEADQUARTERS BUILDING.

The Headquarters of the Convention will be located in the Armory, which is situated on University Street, immediately in the rear of Osgoode Hall, and within two minutes' walk of Queen Street, one of the main thoroughfares of the city. It is easily reached by Yonge and Queen Street cars. The Armory is the largest structure of the kind in Canada, the floor space being 125 feet wide by about 300 feet long. The span of the roof is equal to the width of the floor. The building is what is known as the "modern renaissance" style of architecture, and is constructed of red pressed brick, with limestone trimmings. At each corner, and over the southern entrance, are battlemented towers, which impart an imposing as well as a military appearance to the building. Its construction began in 1891, and the military authorities took possession about two years ago. The Armory is used as drill-room for several regiments.

No meetings will be held here during the Convention, as the acoustic properties are not good, but the work of registration will all be done in this building.

REGISTRATION ARRANGEMENTS

are in charge of Mr. B. N. Davis, who is making careful preparation to handle, without confusion, the large numbers that are expected. Delegates are requested to report at Headquarters immediately on their arrival in the city, when they will be assigned to their homes. Those who have secured accommodation in hotels, etc., before reaching Toronto, are requested not to fail to register at Headquarters, so that a complete record may be kept of the attendance.

The Registration Committee have arranged to have the Registration Headquarters supplied with post-office, telegraph and telephone accommodation. The balance of the space will be provided with tables, chairs and writing material for the convenience of the delegates. Provision is being made to have registration clerks in attendance night and day for the first two days at least.

MASSEY MUSIC HALL.

The largest of the Convention Auditoriums is the Massey Hall. This is a magnificent structure, presented to the citizens of Toronto by the late Hart A. Massey, Esq., who, by the way, was one of the leading Methodists of the city. The exterior is of plain design, in order that the

THE PAVILION.

interior might be constructed to the best advantage for large audiences. The seating capacity of the hall is four thousand, and it is possible to crowd another thousand into the building by using extra seats. It is well ventilated, beautifully lighted by electricity, and altogether is a model place for holding Convention meetings. The architect is Mr. S. R. Badgely, of Cleveland, who designed the Epworth Memorial Church of that city.

METROPOLITAN METHODIST CHURCH.

THE PAVILION.

What is known as the Pavilion is situated in the Horticultural Gardens. It is capable of accommodating an audience of 2,500. Previous to the erection of Massey Hall it was the largest hall in the city, and all big gatherings were held in it. Attached to the Pavilion is a palm house and a conservatory, which may be inspected.

FIRST METHODIST CHURCH, TORONTO,
On present site of Bank of Commerce, corner King and Jordan streets.

THE CHURCHES.

Toronto might well be termed the "City of Churches," as it has nearly two hundred places of worship. Many of these are spacious and beautiful, but the Metropolitan Methodist Church is *facile princeps*. It is a handsome edifice standing in the centre of a square of land that is one of the most valuable in the city. The auditorium will seat an audience of 2,500 persons, but on special occasions more than this number have been crowded into it. Altogether it is a church property that is unequalled in worldwide Methodism.

NEW RICHMOND CHURCH.

Two very short blocks farther east is Cooke's Presbyterian Church, the largest, so far as accommodation for an audience is concerned, of that denomination in Canada. It has a seating capacity about equal to that of the Metropolitan. The auditorium is exceedingly comfortable, and so well planned that every individual can see and hear perfectly. Our Presbyterian friends have kindly granted the Convention the use of this fine building.

COOKE'S CHURCH (PRESBYTERIAN).

Bond Street Congregational Church is a spacious building one block from the Metropolitan, in which some of the Convention meetings will be held.

There are many fine Methodist churches scattered throughout the city. Among them may be mentioned Trinity, Parkdale, Broadway Tabernacle, Carlton Street, Sherbourne Street, Elm Street, New Richmond and Queen Street.

BROADWAY TABERNACLE.

SHERBOURNE STREET CHURCH.

PARKDALE CHURCH.

TRINITY CHURCH.

CARLTON STREET CHURCH.

PROGRAMME.

NOTE.—The figures after the speaker's name indicate the time allotted for the address.

GENERAL TOPIC—"Christ in the World To-day."

OPENING DAY.

Thursday, July 15th.

2.30 P.M.—MASSEY HALL. Chairman, J. L. Hughes, Esq., Toronto.
Devotions, Rev. Chancellor Burwash, Toronto.

ADDRESSES OF WELCOME—

On behalf of the Province and City, Hon. A. S. Hardy, Premier of Ontario. - - - - - - (20)
Singing.
On behalf of Canadian Methodism, Rev. A. Carman, D.D., Toronto. - - - - - - - (20)
Singing.

RESPONSES—

For Methodist Episcopal Church, Bishop W. X. Ninde, LL.D.(20)
For Methodist Episcopal Church South, Bishop O. P. Fitzgerald, Nashville, Tenn. - - - - - (20)
Singing.
For Wesley Guild of England, Rev. Simpson Johnson, Manchester, England. - - - - - - (20)

2.30 P.M.—METROPOLITAN CHURCH. Chairman, J. J. Maclaren, Esq., Q.C., Toronto.
Devotions, Rev. A. C. Courtice, B.D., Toronto, Ont.

ADDRESSES OF WELCOME—

On behalf of the City, Mayor R. J. Fleming. - - (20)
Singing.
On behalf of Toronto Methodism, Rev. William Briggs, D.D., Toronto. - - - - - - - (20)
Singing.

RESPONSES—
    For Methodist Episcopal Church, Bishop C. C. McCabe, LL.D.
                                                                                           (20)
    For Methodist Episcopal Church South, Rev. James Thomas,
        Little Rock, Ark. - - - - - - (20)
    Singing.
    For India, Rev. H. A. Crane, D.D., Bombay, India. - (20)

8.00 P.M.—METROPOLITAN CHURCH. Chairman, W. E. H. Massey,
    Esq., Toronto, Ont.
    Devotions, Rev. Dr. Ryckman, Kingston, Ont.
    Lecture, Bishop John P. Newman, LL.D.
        Subject—"Around the Footstool."

8.00 P.M.—COOKE'S CHURCH. Chairman, Bishop W. X. Ninde, D.D.,
    LL.D.
    Devotions, Rev. S. P. Cresaps, Maryville, Mo.
    Lecture, Bishop Chas. H. Fowler, LL.D.
        Subject—"Great Deeds of Great Men."

8.00 P.M.—MASSEY HALL. Chairman, Rev. W. F. McMurray, Richmond, Mo.

    PLATFORM MEETING—
    Devotions, Rev. John H. Race, Binghampton, N.Y.
    Address, Rev. Wm. I. Haven, D.D., Brookline, Mass.   (30)
        Subject—"Red and White."
    Singing.
    Address, Rev. J. E. Lanceley, Brampton, Ont. - - (30)
        Subject—"What Meaneth this Host?"
    Singing.
    Address, Rev. W. D. Bradfield, Galveston, Tex. - (30)

8.00 P.M.—HORTICULTURAL PAVILION. Chairman, Rev. L. H.
    Murlin, D.D., Baldwin, Kansas.

    PLATFORM MEETING—
    Devotions, Rev. M. H. Ewers, Tuscola, Ill.
    Address, Hon. C. E. Piper, Chicago, Ill. - - - (30)
    Singing.
    Address, Rev. J. V. Smith, D.D., Hamilton, Ont. - (30)
        Subject—"The Good Angel of Life."
    Singing.
    Address, Rev. J. W. Hill, Gainesville, Tex. - - (30)

SECOND DAY.

Friday, July 16th.

6.30 to 7.30 a.m.—METROPOLITAN CHURCH. Sunrise Prayer Meeting, Rev. A. B. Riker, D.D., Charleston, W. Va., Leader.

6.30 to 7.30 a.m.—ELM STREET METHODIST CHURCH. Sunrise Prayer Meeting, Rev. T. B. Clifford, Water Valley, Miss., Leader.

DEPARTMENTAL CONFERENCES.

9.30 a.m.—MASSEY HALL. Department of Spiritual Work.
Conducted by Rev. G. S. Clendinnen, Ottawa, Ont.
Devotions, Rev. M. J. Cofer, Carrollton, Ga.
Address—"The Devotional Leader,"
   Rev. H. M. Dubose, Jackson, Miss. - (10)
Address—"The Devotional Topic,"
   Mr. C. E. German, Strathroy, Ont. - (10)
Discussion - - - - - - - - (15)
Singing.
Address—"Personal Work in the Chapter,"
   Miss Grace Putnam, Chattanooga, Tenn. (10)
Address—"Revival Work in the Chapter,"
   Charles O. Stannard, St. Louis, Mo. - (10)
Discussion - - - - - - - - (15)
Singing.
Address—"Spiritual Work in the Colored Chapters,"
   Rev. Frank Gary, Galveston, Texas. - (10)
Address—"Cottage and School House Prayer Meetings,"
   Rev. J. O. Knott, Washington, D.C.
Question Drawer, Rev. T. B. Neely, Philadelphia, Pa. (15)

9.30 a.m. METROPOLITAN CHURCH. Department of Literary Work.
Conducted by Rev. T. J. Parr, B.A., Merritton, Ont.
Devotions, Rev. J. M. Melear, B.D., Athens, Tenn.
Address—"Books and Reading,"
   Mr. J. Macdonald Oxley, Montreal, Que. (10)
Address—"Value of Literary Work in the League,"
   Rev. Jas. G. Campbell, Ph.D., Delphi, Ind. (10)
Discussion - - - - - - - - (15)
Singing.

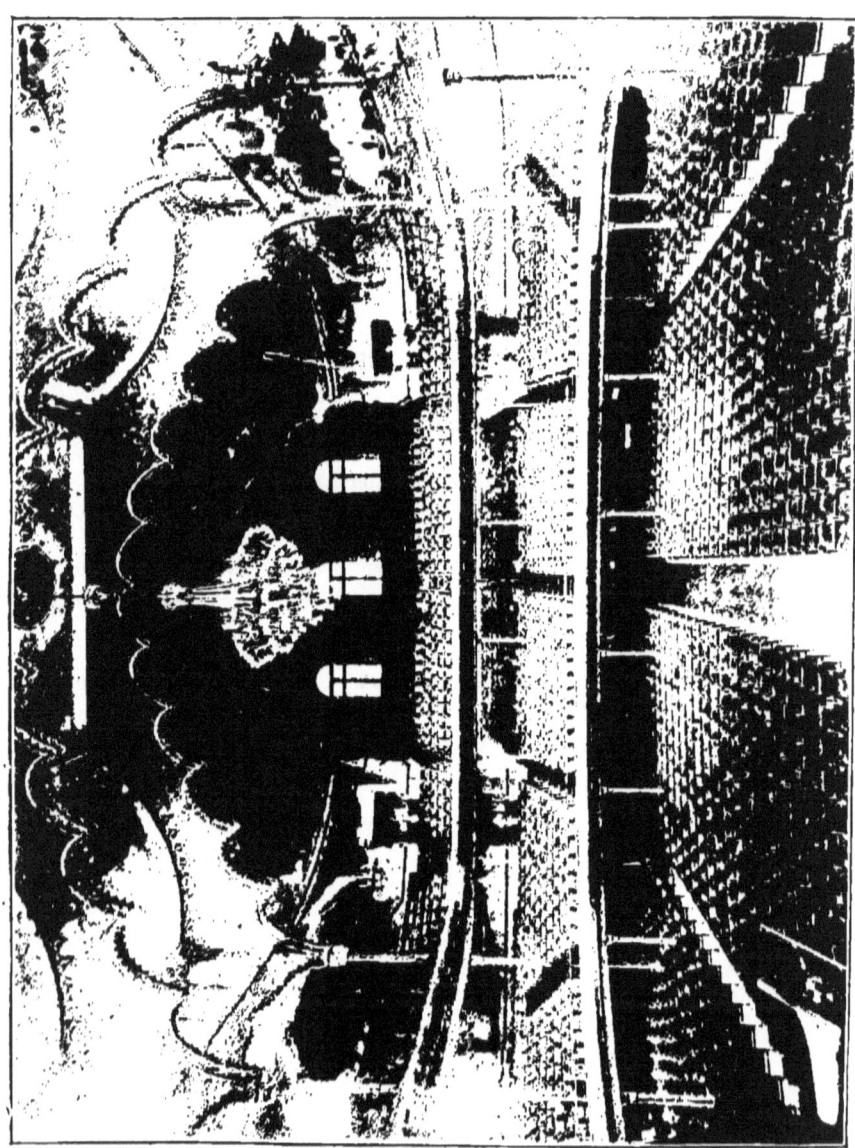

Address—"Methods of Literary Work,"
Prof. H. M. Snyder, Spartanburg, S.C. (10)
Address—"Epworth League Reading Course,"
Mr. A. M. Schoyer, Pittsburg, Pa. - (10)
Discussion - - - - - - - - (15)
Singing.
Address—"Literary Work in Epworth Assemblies,"
Mr. Elvin Swarthout, Grand Rapids, Mich. (10)
Address—"Lectures and Lecture Courses,"
Hon. Wm. L. Woodcock, Altoona, Pa. (10)
Address—"How to Manage a Reading Circle,"
Mr. H. A. Schroetter, Covington, Ky. (10)
Question Drawer, Robert E. Doherty, Ph.D., New York. (15)

9.30 A.M.—COOKE'S CHURCH. Department of SOCIAL WORK.
Conducted by Mr. G. N. Hart, Pine Bluff, Ark.
Devotions, Rev. J. S. Jones, Knoxville, Tenn.
Address—"Social Life in the Church—Its Importance,"
Mrs. Myra Goodwin Plantz, Appleton, Wis. (10)
Address—"Social Life in the Church—How to Promote It,"
Mr. B. F. Swenerton, Halifax, N.S. - (10)
Discussion - . - - - - - - (15)
Singing.
Address—"The Social Committee—Its Duties,"
Mrs. W. G. Solomon, Macon, Ga. - (10)
Discussion - - - - - - - - (15)
Address—"Prohibited Amusements,"
Rev. Edw. S. Ninde, Detroit, Mich. - (10)
Address—"What Social Entertainments Shall We Substitute for Those We Condemn?"
Rev. S. A. Morse, D.D., Corning, N.Y. (10)
Singing.
Address—"The Spiritual Influence of the Social Department,"
Rev. Z. T. Bennett, Paragould, Ark. - (10)
Question Drawer, Rev. J. J. Redditt, Brampton, Ont. (15)

9.30 A.M.—BOND STREET CONGREGATIONAL CHURCH. Department of FINANCE.
Conducted by B. L. Paine, M.D., Lincoln, Neb.
Devotions, Rev. S. Fellery, B.D., Guelph, Ont.
Address—"Systematic Giving,"
Mr. W. O. Whittle, Knoxville, Tenn. - (10)
Address—"The Church Benevolences,"
Rev. W. L. McDowell, D.D., Baltimore, Md. (10)
Discussion - - - - - - - - (15)
Singing.

Address—"Christian Stewardship,"
    Rev. W. B. Beauchamp, Richmond, Va. (10)
Address—"The Tenth Legion,"
    Fred. E. Tasker, Washington, D.C. - (10)
Discussion - - - - - - - - - (15)
Singing.
Address—"League Finances,"
    Rev. J. T. Pate, D.D., Camden, S.C. - (10)
Address—"The Duties of the Treasurer,"
    Miss F. Lazier, Belleville, Ont. - - (10)
Question Drawer, Rev. E. H. Rawlings, Richmond, Va. (15)

9.30 A.M.—THEATRE OF NORMAL SCHOOL (at head of Bond Street).
    —Department of MERCY AND HELP.
Conducted by Rev. S. H. Werlein, St. Louis, Mo.
Devotions, Rev. Ervin L. Thorpe, D.D., Bridgeport, Conn.
Address—"How to Help the Poor,"
    Rev. Willard T. Perrin, Boston, Mass. (10)
Address—"How to Prevent Poverty,"
    Rev. C. E. Dowman, D.D., Columbus, Ga. (10)
Discussion - - - - - - - - - (15)
Singing.
Address—"How to Visit the Sick,"
    Miss Scott, Toronto. - - - - (10)
Address—"Jail Work,"
    Miss Florence Haythorne, Austin, Ill. - (10)
Discussion - - - - - - - - - (15)
Singing.
Address—"Systematic Visitation,"
    Miss S. Bowes, Victoria, B.C. - - (10)
Address—"The King's Daughters,"
    Miss C. May Engle, Germantown, Pa. - (10)
Question Drawer,
    Rev. Paul C. Curnick, S.T.B., Springfield, O. - (15)

9.30 A.M.—CARLTON STREET CHURCH. Department of CORRESPONDENCE.
Conducted by Byron E. Helman, Cleveland, Ohio.
Devotions, Rev. J. R. Barcus, Temple, Texas.
Address—"The Duties of the Secretary,"
    Rev. C. H. Huestis, Barrington, N.S. - (10)
Address—"The Chapter Records,"
    Rev. Geo. W. Switzer, LaFayette, Ind. (10)
Discussion - - - - - - - - - (15)
Singing.

Address—"Correspondence with Absent Members,"
  Mr. Geo. L. Hackney, Asheville, N.C.
Address—"Pulpit Notices,"
  Geo. C. Baker, Camden, N.J. - - (10)
Discussion - - - - - - - - (15)
Singing.
Address—"Communications—What to do with them,"
  Rev. H. E. Foss, A.M., Bangor, Me. - (10)
Address—"How to Advertise the League,"
  Mr. I. E. Brock, Chatham, Ont. - - (10)
Question Drawer, Rev. J. C. Orr, Cleveland, Tenn. - (15)

9.30 A.M.—ELM STREET CHURCH. THE JUNIOR LEAGUE.
Conducted by Frank R. Barbour, Evansville, Ind.
Devotions, Rev. C. W. Watch, Brighton, Ont.
Address—"The Ideal Junior Superintendent,"
  Mrs. Annie E. Smiley, Milford, Mass. (10)
Address—"The Place of the Junior League in the Church,"
  Miss Florence M. Campbell, Suffolk, Va. (10)
Discussion - - - - - - - - (15)
Singing.
Address—"Temperance in the Junior League,"
  Rev. T. Albert Moore, Palmerston, Ont. (10)
Address—"Missions in the Junior League,"
  Miss Libbie R. Hamsher, Monmouth, Ill. (10)
Discussion - - - - - - - - (15)
Singing.
Address—"Junior League Course of Study,"
  Miss Ida L. Martin, Pittsburg, Pa. - (15)
Address—"How Shall we Teach the Juniors to Pray and Testify in Public,"
  Rev. R. S. Boyns, Modesto, Cal. - (10)
Question Drawer, Miss Julia A. Robinson, Dubuque, Ia. (15)

9.30 A.M.—KNOX CHURCH. MISSIONARY CONFERENCE.
Conducted by Willis W. Copper, Kenosha, Wis.
Devotions, Rev. Z. A. Parker, Athens, Ala.
Address—"Students' Volunteer Movement,"
  Miss Ruth Sites, Foochow, China (15)
Address—"Students' Missionary Campaign."
  Rev. D. Norman, B.A., Aurora, Ont. (10)
Discussion - - - - - - - - (15)
Singing.
Address—"A Message from the Field,"
  Rev. E. H. Richards, D.D., Norwalk, Ohio. (15)

Address—"The Missionary Evening in the League,"
        Rev. J. E. Harrison, San Antonio, Tex. (10)
Discussion - - - - - - - - (15)
Singing.
Address—" Missionary Literature and its Circulation,"
        Rev. F. E. Day, Sibley, Iowa. - - (10)
Address—" Methods of Missionary Giving,"
        Rev. C. L. Nye, Perry, Iowa. - - (10)
Question Drawer, Mr. F. C. Stephenson, Toronto, Ont. (15)

EPWORTH RECTORY.

Friday Afternoon, July 16th.

TOPIC—"CHRIST FOR THE WORLD."

Subject.	Massey Hall.	Pavilion.	Metropolitan Church.	Cooke's Church.
Chairman	Bishop J. M. Walden.	Mr. R. M. Kelley, Longview, Tex.	Rev. R. N. Burns, B.A., Toronto, Ont.	Rev. E. S. Osbon, D.D., Yonkers, N.Y.
Devotions	Rev. J. W. Newman, Birmingham, Ala.	Rev. S. O. Royal, Troy, N.Y.	Rev. J. B. Albrook, D.D., Marshalltown, Ia.	Rev. G. H. Cobbledick, D.D., Glencoe, Ont.
"Christ in Personal Experience."	Rev. S. T. Westhafer, Chattanooga, Tenn.	Rev. S. G. Bland, B.A., Smith's Falls, Ont.	Mr. Joe Ramsey, Viola, Tenn.	Mr. Frederick T. Keeney, Elmira, N.Y.
"Christ in the Home."	Rev. J. H. Riddell, B.D., Winnipeg, Man.	Rev. J. F. Stout, D.D., St. Paul, Minn.	R. S. Copeland, M.D., Ann Arbor, Mich.	Miss Emma Tucker, Atlanta, Ga.
"Christ in Business."	Mr. D. G. Bickers, Gainesville, Ga.	Rev. S. J. Herben, New York City.	Mr. Fred. Daly, London, Ont.	Rev. J. W. Mahood, Webster City, Ia.
"Christ in Politics."	F. D. Fuller, Esq., Topeka, Kan.	Mr. Bruce L. Rice, Clarksville, Tenn.	Rev. W. R. Slutz, D.D., Wichita, Kan.	Dr. A. W. Thornton, Chatham, Ont.
"Christlikeness in Spirit and Service."	Rev. W. Sparling, B.A., Quebec, Que.	Rev. W. H. Jordan, D.D., Sioux Falls, S.D.	Rev. M. C. B. Mason, D.D. Cincinnati, Ohio.	Rev. J. A. Rice, Columbia, S.C.
"The Missionary Impulse and Motive."	Rev. Chas. B. Mitchell, Minneapolis, Minn.	Rev. G. F. Salton, Ph.D., St. Thomas, Ont.	Rev. W. J. Carpenter, Orlando, Fla.	Rev. J. C. Murray, D.D., South Atlanta, Ga.

Fifteen minutes will be allowed for each of these Addresses.

Missionary Meetings, Friday Evening, July 16th.

TOPIC—"THE WORLD FOR CHRIST."

At 8 p.m.	Massey Hall.	Pavilion.	Metropolitan Church.	Cooke's Church.
Chairman........	Rev. J. D. Hammond, Macon, Ga.	Rev. S. W. Gehrett, D.D. Philadelphia, Pa.	Rev. E. H. Dewart, D.D., Toronto, Ont.	Bishop John F. Hurst, Washington, D.C.
Devotions	Rev. J. VanCleve, Mt. Vernon, Ill.	Rev. J. W. Shoaff, Selma, Ala.	Rev. L. S. Rader, Jacksonville, Fla.	Rev. D. S. Houck, Picton, Ont.
Address	Rev. A. Sutherland, D.D. Toronto, Ont.	Rev. J. Henderson, D.D. Toronto, Ont.	Rev. W.F.McDowell,D.D. Denver, Col.	Rev. A. Coke Smith, D.D. Lynchburg, Va.
	Singing	Singing	Singing	Singing.
Address	Rev. W.P.Thirkield,D.D. Atlanta, Ga.	Rev. J.P. McFerrin, D.D. Louisville, Ky.	Rev. G. W. Briggs, Owensboro', Ky.	Lecture on Africa, By Bishop Walden.
	Singing	Singing	Singing	
Address	Rev. J.M. Buckley, D.D. New York	Rev. A. J. Palmer, D.D. New York	Rev. J.W. Hamilton, D.D. Cincinnati, O.	

Thirty minutes will be allowed for each of these Addresses. Bishop Walden to have one hour.

THIRD DAY.

Saturday, July 17th.

CHURCH RALLIES.

9.30 to 11.30 A.M.—MASSEY HALL. For Methodist Episcopal Church.
    Chairman, Rev. Arthur Edwards, D.D., Chicago, Ill.
    Devotions, Rev. John H. Coleman, D.D., Albany, N.Y.
    ADDRESSES—
        "The American University,"
            Bishop John F. Hurst, D.D., LL.D., Washington, D.C. - - - - - - (20)
        "Our Publishing Interests,"
            Rev. Homer Eaton, D.D., New York City - (20)
        "The Forward Movement among our Colored Young People,"
            Irvine G. Penn, Atlanta, Ga. - - - - (15)
        "Woman's Work in the Home Church,"
            Mrs. Clinton B. Fisk, New York City. - (15)
        "Woman's Work in Foreign Lands,"
            Bishop C. C. McCabe, LL.D. . - - - (15)

9.30 to 11.30 A.M.—METROPOLITAN CHURCH. For Methodist Episcopal Church South.
    Chairman, Bishop W. W. Duncan, Spartanburg, S.C.
    Devotions, Rev. J. B. Ley, Tallahassee, Fla.
    ADDRESSES—
        Rev. J. J. Tigert, D.D., Nashville, Tenn.
        Rev. Alonzo Monk, D.D., Macon, Ga.
        Rev. W. P. Murrah, Jackson, Miss.
        Bishop J. F. Hurst, Washington, D.C.

9.30 to 11.30 A.M.—COOKE'S CHURCH. For Methodist Church, Canada.
    Chairman, Rev. A. Carman, D.D., General Superintendent.
    Devotions, Rev. J. B. Saunders, M.D., D.D., Ottawa, Ont.
    Chairman's Remarks - - - - - - (10)
    General Secretary's Report - - - - - (20)
    ADDRESSES—
        "Forward Evangelistic Movement,"
            Rev. G. W. Kerby, B.A. - - - (10)
        "Epworth League Reading Course,"
            Mr. A. T. Cooper, Clinton, Ont. - - - (10)
        "Our Publishing Interests,"
            Rev. Dr. Briggs, Toronto, Ont. - - (15)
        "Our Missionary Work,"
            Rev. A. Sutherland, D.D., Toronto, Ont. - (15)
        "Our Educational Work,"
            Rev. John Potts, D.D., Toronto, Ont. - - (15)

OPEN AIR MEETING, SATURDAY AFTERNOON, JULY 17th.
EXHIBITION GROUNDS.

2.30 P.M.—Grand Lacrosse Match (Canada's National Game).
Flag Drill.
National airs by Band of the Royal Grenadiers.
Singing by a large chorus.

4 P.M.— PATRIOTIC SERVICE—
Chairman, Governor Geo. W. Atkinson, LL.D., Charleston, W.Va.
Devotions, Bishop E. R. Hendrix, Kansas City, Mo.
ADDRESSES—
Rev. John Potts, D.D., Toronto, Ont. - - - (20)
Governor D. H. Hastings, Harrisburg, Pa. - - - (20)
Rev. Simpson Johnson, Manchester, England - - (20)

A charge of 25 cents will be made for the afternoon exercises, the proceeds to be devoted to Convention expenses. Get tickets at the Ticket Office in the Armory, and avoid delay at the Grounds.

If the day should happen to be rainy, this meeting will be held in Massey Hall.

To reach the Exhibition Grounds, take King Street West car.

TEMPERANCE AND CIVIC RIGHTEOUSNESS.

8.00 P.M.—MASSEY HALL.
Chairman, Charles R. Magee, Boston, Mass.
Devotions, Rev. M. Dargan, Greeenwood, S.C.
ADDRESSES—
Rev. W. F. Wilson, Toronto, Ont. - - - - (20)
Prof. Samuel Dickie, Albion, Mich. - - - - (20)
Rev. D. C. Kelley, Columbia, Tenn. - - - - (20)

8.00 P.M.—METROPOLITAN CHURCH. Chairman, J. W. Flavelle, Esq., Toronto.
Devotions, Rev. J. W. E. Bowen, D.D., Atlanta, Ga.
Address, Rev. D. H. Moore, D.D., Cincinnati, O. - (25)
Singing.
Address, Rev. W. B. Palmore, D.D., St. Louis, Mo. - (25)
Singing.
Address, Rev. Charles H. Payne, LL.D., New York City (25)

8.00 P.M.—COOKE'S CHURCH. Chairman, Mr. B. N. Davis, Toronto.
Devotions, Rev. J. O. Knott, Washington, D.C.
ADDRESSES—
Ald. F. S. Spence, Toronto, Ont.
Rev. Cladius B. Spencer, D.D., Denver, Col.
Rev. Dr. A. J. Kynett, Philadelphia, Pa.

FOURTH DAY.

Sunday, July 18th.

11.00 A.M.—Sermons in Toronto churches. (See Appointments.)

3.00 P.M.—Love Feast Services—
 METROPOLITAN CHURCH, led by Rev. J. M. Stuart, D.D., Carthage, Mo.
 ELM STREET CHURCH, led by F. W. Tunnell, Germantown, Pa.
 SHERBOURNE STREET CHURCH, led by Rev. Dr. Griffith, Brockville, Ont.
 BROADWAY TABERNACLE, led by Rev. Matthew G. Coleman, Beardstown, Ill.
 QUEEN STREET CHURCH, led by Rev. J. A. Wailes, St. Charles, Mo.
 PARKDALE CHURCH, led by O. L. Doty, Cleveland, Ohio.
 CENTRAL CHURCH, led by Rev. G. J. Bishop, Toronto.
 TRINITY CHURCH, led by Rev. J. R. Creighton, D.D., Stevens Point, Wis.
 WOODGREEN CHURCH, led by Rev. G. W. Young, Richmond, Ky.

3.00 P.M.—Communion Services—
 CARLTON STREET CHURCH, conducted by Rev. Wm. B. Leach, D.D., Chicago, Ill.
 BERKELEY STREET CHURCH, conducted by Rev. John Stephens, San Francisco, Cal.

JUNIOR LEAGUE RALLY.

3.00 P.M.—MASSEY HALL. Chairman, Mrs. Mary C. Foster, New York City.
 Devotions.
 ADDRESSES—
  Rev. S. T. Bartlett, Cobourg, Ont. - - - - (15)
  Mrs. Perry E. Powell, Anderson, Ind. - - - (15)
  Rev. Chas. O. Jones, Chattanooga, Tenn. - - - (15).
 SOLOS—By Masters Claude Saner and Berney Rautenberg.

7.00 P.M.—Regular services in all the churches. (See Appointments.)

FAREWELL MEETINGS.

8.30 P.M. —MASSEY HALL. Chairman, Rev. James Atkins, Nashville, Tenn.
    Devotions, Rev. Willis P. Odell, Ph.D., Buffalo, N.Y.
    Address—" Equipment for Service,"
        Rev. Herbert F. Briggs, San Jose, Cal.
    Address—" Baptism of Power,"
        Rev. S. P. Rose, D.D., Montreal, Que.   (15)
    Farewell Address, followed by Consecration Service,
        Rev. J. H. Hollingsworth, Greencastle, Ind.

8.30 P.M. METROPOLITAN CHURCH. Chairman, Rev. J. F. Berry, D.D., Chicago.
    Devotions, Rev. G. T. Adams, B.D., Nashville, Tenn.
    Address—" Equipment for Service,"
        Rev. G. M. Campbell, Charlottetown, P.E.I.(15)
    Address—" Baptism of Power,"
        Rev. E. B. Ramsey, Memphis, Tenn.   (15)
    Farewell Address, followed by Consecration Service,
        Rev. Manly S. Hard, D.D., Kingston, Pa.

8.30 P.M.—COOKE'S CHURCH. Chairman, Rev. Wm. D. Parr, Kokomo, Ind.
    Devotions, Rev. G. R. Turk, Winnipeg, Man.
    Address—" Equipment for Service,"
        Rev. Geo. W. Brown, D.D., North Adams, Mass. (15)
    Address—" Baptism of Power,"
        Rev. W. F. Hamner, Memphis, Tenn.   (15)
    Consecration Service, led by the Chairman.

8.30 P.M.—HORTICULTURAL PAVILION.—Chairman, Mr. J. R. L. Starr, Toronto.
    Devotions, Rev. Leslie J. Naftzger, Muncie, Ind.
    Address—" Equipment for Service,"
        Rev. Edwin H. Hughes, Malden, Mass.   (15)
    Address—" The Baptism of Power,"
        Rev. W. K. Piner, Bowling Green, Ky.   (15)
    Farewell Address, followed by Consecration Service,
        Rev. Madison Swadener, Cincinnati, Ohio.

8.30. P.M.—BROADWAY TABERNACLE.
Chairman, Rev. B. F. Fraser, Elberton, Ga.
Devotions, Rev. Clarence O. Kimball, Ph.D., St. Elmo, Ill.
ADDRESSES—
"Equipment for Service,"
Rev. C. T. Scott, B.A., St. Thomas, Ont. (15)
"Baptism of Power,"
Rev. J. M. Thoburn, jun., Detroit, Mich.
Farewell Address, followed by Consecration Service,
Rev. A. H. Ranton, Kalamazoo, Mich.

IMPORTANT INFORMATION FOR DELEGATES.

1. All evening meetings will be preceded by a half-hour Song Service, commencing at 7.30.

2. Restaurants and refreshment booths will be established at the Armory Building and Massey Hall.

3. The Convention Badge will be the ticket of admission to all the services. Only Badge-holders will be admitted up to within 15 minutes of commencing the meeting. After that the doors will be open to the general public.

4. The Convention Badge will be supplied, without charge, with the Souvenir Programme, which will be sold for 25 cents. The only way to get the Badge is to purchase the Programme.

5. Arrangements have been made with the Canadian Customs Department to put on a special force of examiners at Toronto, to facilitate the examination of delegates' baggage. Delegates should therefore check their baggage through to Toronto in bond.

6. Visitors will find the map on the back of this book a convenience in locating places of interest. The Convention buildings are marked by plain red blocks.

NATIONAL CONFERENCE OF CHARITIES.

The Twenty-fourth National Conference of Charities and Correction will meet in Toronto during the week preceding the opening of the Epworth League meeting. This Conference, which is composed of leading workers in charitable and prison reform work, will be of a thoroughly interesting and practical character, and all who are engaged in philanthropic effort will receive great benefit from these meetings. The opening session will be held in the Pavilion, on Wednesday evening, July 7th, and the subsequent meetings will be held in the Normal School. The afternoons will be devoted to sections for charity organization, child-saving, prison reform, county and municipal charities, etc. Mr. Alex. Johnson, of Fort Wayne, Indiana, is President, and Mr. H. H. Hart, of St. Paul, Minn., General Secretary. A strong local committee has been formed, and all the hospitality of the city will be extended to visitors. Reduced railway and hotel rates have been arranged for.

GRAND STAND, EXHIBITION GROUNDS.

Plan of Appointments for Regular Sunday Services.

METHODIST.

Metropolitan—
    11 A.M.—Rev. J. F. Berry, D.D., Chicago, Ill.
    7 P.M.—Rev. Simpson Johnson, Manchester, England.

Sherbourne Street—
    11 A.M.—Bishop O. P. Fitzgerald, Nashville, Tenn.
    7 P.M.—Bishop Chas. H. Fowler, D.D., LL.D.

Trinity (Cor. Bloor and Robert streets)—
    11 A.M.—Bishop John P. Newman, D.D., LL.D.
    7 P.M.—Rev. J. M. Buckley, D.D., New York City.

Elm Street—
    11 A.M.—Rev. A. J. Palmer, D.D., New York City.
    7 P.M.—Bishop C. C. McCabe, D.D., LL.D.

Parkdale—
    11 A.M.—Rev. E. B. Ramsey, Memphis, Tenn.
    7 P.M.—Bishop J. M. Walden, D.D.

Carlton Street—
    11 A.M.—Bishop W. X. Ninde, D.D., LL.D.
    7 P.M.—Rev. Charles B. Mitchell, D.D., Minneapolis, Minn.

Broadway Tabernacle (Cor. Spadina Ave and College Street)—
    11 A.M.—Bishop Hendrix, Kansas City, Mo.
    7 P.M.—Rev. E. B. Patterson, D.D., Jamestown, N.Y.

Queen Street—
    11. A.M.—Rev. W. T. Perrin, Boston, Mass.
    7 P.M.—Rev. A. C. Hirst, D.D., Chicago, Ill.

Berkeley Street—
    11 A.M.—Bishop W. W. Duncan.
    7. P.M.—Rev. J. H. Coleman, D.D., Albany, N.Y.

Central (Bloor Street)—
    11 A.M.—Bishop John F. Hurst, D.D., Washington, D.C.
    7 P.M.—Rev. W. K. Thirkield, D.D., Atlanta, Ga.

McCaul Street (Near Queen)—
    11 A.M.—Rev. E. S. Ninde, Detroit, Mich.
    7 P.M.—Rev. J. A. Rice, D.D., Columbia, S.C.

St. Paul's (Avenue Road)—
    11 A.M.—Rev. J. VanCleve, D.D., Mount Vernon, Ill.
    7 P.M.—Rev. C. H. Payne, D.D., New York City.

Wesley (Dundas Street)—
  11 A.M.—Rev. J. H. Potts, D.D., Detroit, Mich.
  7 P.M.—Rev. A. Coke Smith, Lynchburg, Va.

Euclid Avenue—
  11 A.M.—Rev. E. L. Thorpe, Bridgeport, Conn.
  7 P.M.—Rev. M. C. B. Mason, D.D., Cincinnati, O.

Bathurst Street—
  11 A.M.—Mrs. Annie E. Smiley, Milford, Mass.
  7 P.M.—Rev. I. B. Scott, New Orleans, La.

Clinton Street—
  11 A.M.—Rev. T. B. Clifford, Water Valley, Miss.
  7 P.M.—Rev. D. C. Kelley, Columbia, Tenn.

St. Alban's (Parkdale)—
  11 A.M.—Rev. M. J. Cofer, Gainesville, Ga.
  7 P.M.—Rev. M. H. Ewers, Tuscola, Ill.

Parliament Street—
  11 A.M.—Rev. E. H. Rawlings, Richmond, Va.
  7 P.M.—Rev. Paul C. Curnick, Springfield, O.

Woodgreen (Queen Street East)—
  11 A.M.—Dr. R. R. Doherty, New York City.
  7 P.M.—Rev. J. H. Race, Binghamton, N.Y.

Gerrard Street—
  11 A.M.—Rev. W. F. McMurray, Richmond, Mo.
  7 P.M.—Rev. S. O. Royal, Troy, O.

Simpson Avenue—
  11 A.M.—Rev. G. W. Switzer, LaFayette, Ind.
  7 P.M.—Rev. J. O. Knott, Washington, D.C.

King Street—
  11 A.M.—Rev. H. C. Weakley, Cincinnati, O.
  7 P.M.—Rev. J. W. Shoaff, Selma, Ala.

Queen Street East—
  11 A.M.—Rev. D. S. Houck, Picton, Ont.

St. Clarens Avenue—
  11 A.M.—Rev. J. R. Barcus, Temple, Tex.
  7 P.M.—Rev. Z. A. Parker, D.D., Athens, Ala.

Agnes Street—
  11 A.M.—Rev. A. B. Riker, D.D., Charleston, W.Va.
  7 P.M.—Rev. J. M. Wilkinson, B.A.

Epworth—
  11 A.M.—Rev. C. H. Huestis, B.A., Barrington, N.S.

Westmoreland Avenue—
  11 A.M.—Rev. J. W. Newman, Birmingham, Ala.
  7 P.M.—Rev. J. T. Pate, D.D., Camden, S.C.

Crawford Street—
>11 A.M.—Mrs. Clinton B. Fisk, New York.
>7 P.M. —Rev. S. P. Cresaps, Maryville, Mo.

B. M. E. Church (Chestnut Street)—
>11 A.M.—Rev. Frank Gary, Galveston, Tex.

PRESBYTERIAN.

Cooke's—
>11 A.M.—Rev. J. P. McFerrin, D.D., Louisville, Ky.
>7 P.M.—Rev. J. W. Hamilton, D.D., Cincinnati, O.

Old St. Andrew's (Jarvis Street)—
>11 A.M.—Rev. C. M. Stuart, Evanston, Ill.
>7 P.M.—Rev. D. H. Murlin, D.D., Baldwin, Kan.

Knox (Queen Street)—
>11 A.M.—Rev. Herbert F. Briggs, D.D., San Jose, Cal.
>7 P.M.—Rev. J. F. Stout, D.D., St. Paul, Minn.

Central—
>11 A.M.—Rev. Homer Eaton, D.D., New York City.
>7 P.M.—Rev. W. H. Jordan, D.D., Sioux City, S.D.

Parkdale (Dunn Avenue)—
>11 A.M.—Rev. F. T. Keeney, Elmira, N.Y.
>7 P.M.—Rev. S. H. Werlein, D.D., St. Louis, Mo.

College Street—
>11 A.M.—Rev. W. K. Piner, Bowling Green, Ky.
>7 P.M.—Rev. J. M. Thoburn, jun., Detroit, Mich.

Bloor Street—
>7 P.M.—Rev. D. H. Moore, D.D., Cincinnati, O.

East Presbyterian (Oak Street)—
>11 A.M.—Rev. James Thomas, Little Rock, Ark.
>7 P.M.—Rev. Geo. W. Brown, D.D., North Adams, Mass.

St. Enoch's—
>11 A.M.—Rev. H. M. Dubose, Jackson, Miss.
>7 P.M.—Rev. Clarence O. Kimball, St. Elmo, Ill.

Erskine—
>11 A.M.—Rev. G. W. Briggs, Owensboro', Ky.

BAPTIST.

Jarvis Street—
>11 A.M.—Rev. Willis P. Odell, D.D., Buffalo, N.Y.
>7 P.M.—Rev. Alonzo Monk, D.D., Macon, Ga.

Walmer Road—
>11 A.M.—Rev. Dr. J. J. Tigert, Nashville, Tenn.
>7 P.M.—Rev. W. I. Haven, D.D., Brookline, Mass.

Bloor Street—
   11 A.M.—Rev. E. S. Osbon, D.D., Yonkers, N.Y.
   7 P.M.—Rev. W. B. Slutz, D.D., Wichita, Kan.
Beverley Street—
   11 A.M.—Rev. W. D. Bradfield, Galveston, Tex.
   7 P.M.—Rev. Jas. G. Campbell, Ph.D., Delphi, Ind.
First Avenue—
   7 P.M.—Platform-meeting, Rev. S. A. Morse, D.D., Corning, N.Y., and Rev. L. S. Rader, D.D., Jacksonville, Fla.
College Street—
   11 A.M.—Rev. S. W. Gehrett, D.D., Philadelphia, Pa.
   7 P.M.—Rev. J. H. Hill, Gainesville, Tex.

CONGREGATIONAL.

Northern (Church Street, near Carlton)—
   11 A.M.—Rev. J. R. Creighton, Stephen's Point, Wis.
   7 P.M.—Rev. J. C. Orr, Cleveland, Tenn.

MASSEY HALL.

Regular Church service, 7 P.M.—Rev. E. M. Mills, Elmira, N.Y.

STATE HEADQUARTERS.

State of Michigan—Bond Street Congregational Church.
State of Indiana—Carlton Street Methodist Church.
State of Iowa—Central Methodist Church, Bloor Street.
State of Illinois—Palmer House.
First General Conference District (including States of Maine, New Hampshire, Vermont, Massachusetts, Rhode Island and Connecticut)—Fred Victor Mission, Corner of Queen and Jarvis streets.
Fourth General Conference District (States of Pennsylvania, West Virginia, Maryland, Delaware, District of Columbia)—Elm Street Methodist Church.
Fifth General Conference District (States of Ohio and Kentucky)—Knox Church, Queen Street.
Genesee Conference (State of New York)—McMaster University, Bloor Street.
Bay of Quinte Conference (Canada)—Sherbourne Street Methodist Church.
Methodist Episcopal Church South (Southern States)—Metropolitan Church.

BIOGRAPHICAL SKETCHES

OF

THOSE WHO WILL TAKE PART IN THE PROGRAMME.

The Committee regret that they are unable to present a biographical sketch of each speaker. In some cases the information arrived too late for publication.

Owing to the large number on the Programme, it has been found impossible to publish portraits of all. The Committee, therefore, have decided to insert photos of Bishops, Epworth League officials, and those in charge of Church Departments.

ADAMS, REV. G. T., B.D., is pastor of the Epworth Church, Nashville, Tenn., and general secretary of the Nashville Leagues. He was born in North Carolina in 1889. For four years he was principal of a school in New Bern, N.C., receiving the degree of B.D. from Vanderbilt University.

ATKINSON, GOVERNOR, was born in Charleston, W. Va., educated at Ohio Wesleyan University and Columbia University. He was postmaster at Charleston for eight years, revenue agent for three years, U. S. Marshall for District of West Virginia for four years. He has also been a member of Congress and editor of the Wheeling *Evening Standard*. He is a member of the Methodist Episcopal Church, and is interested in the Epworth League and church work generally. He is Governor of the State of West Virginia, and resides at Charleston.

BARBOUR, F. M., is a member of a prominent manufacturing firm in Evansville, Ind., and President of the Indiana State Epworth League. He was born in Kentucky, 1850. He has been Superintendent of Trinity M. E. Sunday School for five years, and is now Superintendent of the Trinity Junior League. Mr. Barbour has given special attention to the Junior work, and is a firm believer in training up children in the Methodist Church to be Methodists.

BARCUS, REV. JOHN McFERRIN, is pastor of the First M. E. Church South, Temple, Tex., and Secretary of the North-West Texas Conference. He was born in Arkansas, December 23rd, 1860, and educated at Southwestern University, Georgetown, Tenn., where he took his degree of A.M. in class of 1882. He was a member of the last General Conference held at Memphis, Tenn., being the youngest delegate.

BARTLETT, REV. S. T., is Vice-President of the Junior Department of the Bay of Quinte Conference, Methodist Church, Canada, and a Junior League specialist. He has recently prepared a book on Junior Methods of work, which should be in the hands of every Junior worker who desires to do effective work. It is known as "The Junior League Hand-Book."

BENNETT, REV. Z. T., D.D., is now serving his third year as pastor of the M. E. Church South at Paragould, Ark. He was born in 1849 in Fayette County, Tenn. After teaching for six years he entered the ministry in 1874. Has been Conference Secretary and a delegate to the General Conference. Also for six years was a member of the General Board of Missions. For seven years he was editor of the *Arkansas Methodist*, voluntarily retiring in 1894 for the pastorate.

BERRY, REV. JOSEPH F., D.D., was born at Aylmer, Ont., March 30th, 1856, and was educated at Milton Academy. When only sixteen years of age he began to preach, and was popularly known as the "Boy Preacher." Two years later he was received into the Canadian Conference, and was subsequently transferred to the Methodist Episcopal Church in the United States. After a number of years in the pastorate, spent mostly in the Michigan Conference, he was elected associate editor of the Michigan *Christian Advocate*, filling that position for three years. Upon the founding of the *Epworth Herald*, he was elected as its editor, in which position he has been a great success. The paper has reached a circulation of 105,000, the largest of any denominational paper in the world. In addition to his editorial duties Dr. Berry frequently preaches and lectures in the interests of the Epworth League.

REV. J. F. BERRY, D.D.

BEAUCHAMP, REV. W. B., B.D., is pastor of St. James M. E. Church South, Richmond, Va. He was born at Farnham, Va., in 1869, and graduated at Vanderbilt University, Nashville. He is Vice-President of the Virginia Epworth League, and has given special attention to the Literary Department of League work.

BICKERS, MR. L. G., is Editor-in-Chief of the *Georgia Cracker*, published at Gainesville, Ga. He was born in the State of Virginia, April, 1873, and educated at Emory College, Oxford, Ga. He has followed the pencil ever since he was able to sharpen it, and he has been an active leaguer since the movement began. Mr. Bickers is a member of the First M. E. Church South at Gainesville, and is also President of the Epworth Leagues of the district in which he lives. He has given some special effort to pushing the Department of Worship in the Leagues under his jurisdiction. He occasionally contributes verses to the *Epworth Era*.

BLAND, REV. S. G., B.A., is a son of the Manse, his father being one of the oldest and most esteemed ministers of the Montreal Conference. Mr. Bland was born in Lachute, Que., 1859, educated at Morrin College, Quebec, and McGill College, Montreal, graduating in 1877. He entered the ministry in 1880, and has been stationed at Cataraqui, Farmersville, Kingston, Quebec and Cornwall. At present he is associated with his father in the pastorate of the Methodist Church, Smith's Falls, Ont.

BOWEN, REV. J. W. E., D.D., is Professor in Gammon Theological Seminary, Atlanta, Ga. Was educated at New Orleans University and Boston University. Dr. Bowen has lectured extensively on subjects relative to the education and advancement of the colored people of the South. Is a member of the Epworth League Board of Control of the M. E. Church.

BOWES, MISS S., is a representative of the Metropolitan Methodist Church, Victoria, B.C. She is a prominent worker in the W. C. T. U. in the Province of British Columbia.

BOYNS, ROBERT S., was born in Cornwall, Eng., in 1867, and educated at the Truro Wesleyan College. He is a local preacher, at present supplying the pulpit of the M. E. Church South at Modesto, Cal. For eleven years past he has been Secretary of the Young Men's Christian Association in San Francisco, and is now President of the San Francisco District League of the M. E. Church South.

BRADFIELD, REV. W. D., B.D., is pastor of St. John's Methodist Episcopal Church South, Galveston, Tenn. Was born in 1866 at Daingerfield, and educated at Vanderbilt University.

BRIGGS, REV. G. W., is pastor at Settle Chapel, Owensboro', Ky., and is connected with the M. E. Church South. He was born in Greensboro', Ala., 1851, was educated in the Southern University in the same city, and graduated in 1873 ; joined the Alabama Conference in 1874. Four years later was transferred to the State of Texas, was stationed in St. James Church, Galveston. Has also been stationed at St. John's and Houston, Texas. For four years was editor of the Texas *Christian Advocate*, which position he resigned and was sent to the capital city of the State, Austin, where he remained for four years. From this place he was sent to Owensboro', where he is now stationed.

BRIGGS, REV. HERBERT F., was born in San Francisco, Cal., January 16th, 1859, and took his college course at the Northwestern University, Evanston, Ill. Entered the ministry in California Conference in 1889. He leaves California for two years of special study in Germany and England in June of this year. Before continuing his journey farther east he will stop at Toronto and represent the great Pacific Coast country at the International gathering of the Epworth League.

BRIGGS, REV. WILLIAM, D.D., was born at Banbridge, Ireland, and received his education in Liverpool, England, where he went into business with the largest and wealthiest corn merchants in that city. The training which he there received has been of very great value to him in later years, as he is now occupying the position of Book Steward of the Methodist Church, Canada. He has succeeded in building up a great business, and has made the Methodist Book Room the largest Publishing House in the Dominion, yielding every year a profit of several thousand dollars, which is applied to the Superannuated Ministers' Fund. Previous to his appointment as Book Steward, Dr. Briggs occupied the most prominent pulpits in the denomination. Among them may be mentioned, Toronto, Hamilton, London, Montreal, Cobourg and Belleville. He was taken from the pastorate of the Metropolitan Church, Toronto, when he was elected Book Steward.

REV. WILLIAM BRIGGS, D.D.

BROCK, MR. IVOR E., was born in Wales, 1865 ; arrived in Canada some few years later with his parents. He now has charge of the house furnishing department of a large dry goods store in Chatham, Ont., and is a member of the Victoria Avenue Church. He has been President of his local Epworth League, and is now secretary of the London Conference Epworth League, having been re-elected at the last Convention at St. Thomas.

BROWN, REV. GEORGE W., D.D., was born in Troy, N.Y., 1838, educated at Union College and the School of Theology, Boston University, and is now pastor of the Methodist Episcopal Church of North Adams, Mass., a large church with one thousand members. Has been pastor at Albany, Brandon (Vt.), Gainsville (Ill.), Saratoga Springs, Troy (N.Y.), Glen Falls, Fort Plain (N.Y.). There is a large and flourishing Epworth League connected with his church, also a Junior League of nearly one hundred members.

BUCKLEY, REV. J. M., D.D., is editor of the New York *Christian Advocate*. He was born at Rahway, N.J., December 16th, 1836, educated at Pennington Seminary, New Jersey, and Wesleyan University. Entered the ministry in 1858 in New Hampshire, remained five years in that State, travelled a year in Europe, spent three years in Detroit. Was pastor nine years in Brooklyn and six years in Stamford, Conn. Was elected editor of the *Christian Advocate* in 1880. Has been a member of the General Conference many times, and has always taken a leading part in the discussions. Dr. Buckley is a trustee of Wesleyan University, Drew Theological Seminary and Pennington Seminary, and has been President of the Methodist Episcopal General Hospital of Brooklyn.

REV. J. M. BUCKLEY, D.D.

BURNS, REV. R. N., B.A., is pastor of the Methodist Church, Orillia, Ont. He was born in Shelburne, Ont., in 1856, and graduated from Victoria University in 1879. For some years he has been closely associated with young people's work, having been President of the Ontario Young People's Society, and a member of the General Board of the Epworth League. He was one of the speakers at the Chattanooga Conference.

BURWASH, REV. N., S.T.D., LL.D., Chancellor of Victoria University, Toronto, Ont. Dr. Burwash was born in the Province of Quebec in 1839, graduated in 1859, spent seven years in the pastorate and thirty-one years in college work. Previous to his present appointment he had charge of the Theological Department of Victoria University.

REV. N. BURWASH, S.T.D.

CAMPBELL, REV. G. M., is pastor of the First Methodist Church, Charlottetown, P.E.I. He was born in Wallace, N.S., 1852, and educated at Mount Allison College and the Wesleyan University, Sackville. Became a local preacher when seventeen years of age, and entered the ministry in 1872. He has filled some of the best pulpits in New Brunswick and P. E. I. Conference, among which may be mentioned Woodstock, St. Stephens, Moncton, and St. John. His present church is one of the largest in eastern Canada. Mr. Campbell is president of the Maritime Union Christian Endeavor, and represented the Maritime Provinces at the Inter-Provincial Convention at Ottawa last year. He has been closely connected with Sunday School work in New Brunswick.

CAMPBELL, MISS FLORENCE, resides at Suffolk, Va., and is president of the League and superintendent of the Junior League in Main Street M. E Church South. Miss Campbell was born in Liverpool, England, and was educated at Queen's College in that city. At present she teaches vocal and instrumental music in Suffolk Female College.

CAMPBELL, REV. JAMES G., Ph.D., was born at Gallipolis, Ohio, January 30, 1863, and has been a resident of Indiana since early life. Prior to entering the ministry he was a teacher. He graduated from De Pauw University in 1886, and during his school-days held several positions of honor and trust. He has held important charges in the Northwest Indiana Conference, and is now pastor of the First Methodist Episcopal Church at

Delphi, Ind. He is the efficient Superintendent of Literary Work of the Epworth League of Indiana.

CARPENTER, REV. W. J., is pastor of the M. E. Church South, Orlando, Fla. Was born in Ohio, 1856, entered the ministry in the Southwest Missouri Conference in 1865. He has been presiding elder, the youngest man ever appointed to that office in his Conference, and has given special attention to revival work. At present he is President of the Florida State League.

CARMAN, REV. A., D.D., is General Superintendent of the Methodist Church, Canada. He was born in the township of Matilda, County of Dundas, Ont., June 27th, 1833, and was educated at Dundas County Grammar School, Iroquois, and Victoria University, Cobourg. Entered the ministry of the Methodist Episcopal Church in Canada in 1856. Has been Professor and Principal of Belleville Seminary, President and Chancellor of Albert University, representative to General Conferences of Methodist Episcopal Church, and Bishop of the Methodist Episcopal Church in Canada. He travels over the whole Dominion in pursuance of his official duties.

REV. A. CARMAN, D.D.

CLENDINNEN, REV. GEO. S., B.A., is pastor of the Methodist Church at Billings Bridge, Ont. Was born in Pembroke, Ont., 1866, and educated in McGill University and Wesleyan Theological College, Montreal. He has been Vice-President of the Ontario Methodist Young People's Association, President of the Ottawa Methodist Young People's Union, Fifth Vice-President of the Montreal Epworth League, and Third Vice-President of the Ottawa District Epworth League, which position he now holds.

CLIFFORD, REV. THOS. B., is pastor of the Main Street M. E. Church South, Water Valley, Miss. He is also President of the Mississippi State Conference of Epworth Leagues. Has built four churches and two parsonages during his ministry of five and a half years. He was born in Oxfordshire, England, 1863, was educated in England and holds certificates from the University of Cambridge and Trinity College.

COBBLEDICK, REV. G. H., M.A., B.D., was born in Middlesex County, Ont., 1859, and graduated from Victoria University in 1885. Has been stationed in Brussels, Galt and Glencoe. He has taken a prominent part in young people's work both in the Christian Endeavor Society, and more recently in the Epworth League. Has organized upwards of twenty-five chapters. At present he is First Vice-President of the London Conference League.

COFER, REV. M. J., is presiding elder of the Carrollton District, North Georgia Conference, M. E. Church South, and resides at Carrollton. He is President of the Epworth League Board North Georgia Conference, President of the Widows' and Orphans' Association of his Conference, and trustee of the *Wesleyan Christian Advocate*.

COLEMAN, REV. M. G., is President of the Illinois Conference Epworth League, and pastor of the First M. E. Church at Beardstown, Ill. He was bord at Danville, Ill., 1858, educated at the State University, and entered the ministry in 1888. He attended both the International Conventions at Cleveland and Chattanooga. Has had considerable success as a League organizer.

COOPER, MR. WILLIS W., is President of the Wisconsin State League, and resides at Kenosha. He was General Corresponding Secretary of the Young People's Methodist Alliance, an organization which was actively pushed throughout the West, until at the time of the organization of the Epworth League, the Alliance was the largest Young People's Society in Methodism. Mr. Cooper was given the honor of calling together representatives of the five separate Methodist organizations in the city of Cleveland on the now historical 15th day of May, 1889, when the Epworth League was launched. Mr. Cooper presided through the entire session of this conference. He has served the Epworth League as its first vice-president for the past seven years, retiring at the last session of the General Conference. Mr. Cooper's special interest is in the cause of missions, to which he has consecrated his life. His first noticeable work in this direction was in 1893, when he called upon the members of the Epworth League of his church to lay upon its altars fifty cents per member on Thanksgiving Day as a special thank-offering. Nearly $50,000 was realized for the Missionary Society in response to this call.

COPELAND, R. S., M.D., is Professor in the University of Michigan and a member of the First M. E. Church, Ann Arbor. Was born in Dexter, Mich., 1868, and educated in the University of Michigan, also taking a graduating course abroad. He was a delegate to the last General Conference, and is now a member of the Epworth League Board of Control. Professor Copeland has given special attention to the Literary Department of the League, and has delivered numerous addresses at Epworth League and Sunday School Conventions. He now teaches a Bible class of University students with an average attendance of about one hundred.

COURTICE, REV. A. C., M.A., B.D., editor of the *Christian Guardian*, the official organ of the Methodist Church in Canada. He is a native of Prince Albert, Ontario County, graduated with M.A. from Toronto College and B.D. from Victoria University, and has been stationed at Toronto, London, Montreal and Kingston. He was elected to his present position by the General Conference of 1894.

REV. A. C. COURTICE, M.A., B.D.

CRANE, REV. H. A., M.A., was born at New Haven, Vt., in 1859, and graduated from Syracuse University in 1885; entered the ministry same year in the North Nebraska Conference, labored as pastor and president of the College until 1892, when at Bishop Thoburn's invitation he went to Bombay, India, and took general charge of the Methodist English-speaking churches in that city. In 1896 he was appointed presiding elder of the Bombay District, and served until compelled to return to America on account of the health of his family.

CREIGHTON, REV. J. R., is a Canadian, having been born in London, Ont., in 1838. He is a son of the late Rev. Kennedy Creighton, well known in Canadian Methodism. Mr. Creighton attended Victoria

College and McGill College, Montreal. At first he intended to be a chemist and druggist, but his life plans were changed through the preaching of the late Rev. Dr. Douglas. In 1867 he entered the ministry in the Minnesota Conference. He was secretary of that Conference for ten years. In 1880 he was transferred to Wisconsin where he occupied leading pastorates and served as presiding elder for ten years.

CRESAPS, REV. S. P., was born in St. Charles, Mo., April 26, 1869, educated at Central College and entered the ministry in 1892. He is now pastor of the M. E. Church South, Maryville, Mo., and has been a member of the Executive Committee of the State League since its organization.

CREWS, REV. A. C., is General Secretary of Epworth Leagues and Sunday Schools in the Methodist Church, Canada, to which position he was elected in May, 1895. He was born in the County of Lambton, 1857, and received his education at the Ingersoll High School and Victoria University. After ordination he spent one year as assistant editor of the *Christian Guardian*, and has been stationed in St. Catharines, Hamilton, Winnipeg and Toronto.

REV. A. C. CREWS.

DALY, MR. F. W., is engaged in business at London, Ont., and is a graduate in Arts from Victoria College, Cobourg. Has been President of the Methodist Young People's Association of Ontario. He is now a member of Dundas Street Centre Methodist Church, London, and has given special attention to temperance work.

CURNICK, REV. PAUL C., A.M., was born in Evansville, Indiana, November 15, 1863. Attended school at the Ohio Normal University, finishing his education at Boston University School of Theology. Most of his ministerial work has been done in Boston, Cincinnati and Springfield, O. He has given special attention to the Epworth Guards.

DAVIS, MR. B. N., Toronto, is a lawyer. He is a member of Carlton Street Church, President of the Toronto Union of Epworth Leagues, and a member of the Committee of Arrangements for the International Epworth League Convention, having charge of the Registration Committee.

DAY, REV. F. E., was born in California in 1864, educated at the Iowa State University, and entered the ministry in 1883. At present he is pastor of the M. E. Church, Sibley, Northwest Iowa Conference, one of the largest and strongest churches in the Conference. Mr. Day was a member of the State Cabinet of the Iowa Epworth League from 1892 to 1893, and State President 1895-1896. He is now a member of the Iowa State Epworth League Summer Assembly Commission, which has acquired a fine Epworth Park at Colfax Springs.

DEWART, REV. E. H., D.D., was born in the County of Cavan, Ireland, and came to Canada in 1834. He entered the ministry in 1852, and was ordained in 1855. During his pastorate he was stationed at St. Thomas, Port Hope, Thorold, Dundas and Ingersoll. From the last named place he was called to assume the editorship of the *Christian Guardian*, the official organ of the Methodist Church in Canada. This position he held for twenty-six years, the longest period of service of any editor the *Guardian* has had. He retired from active work two years ago. Dr. Dewart has always been recognized as an able editorial writer, and has also published a volume of poems of considerable merit.

DICKIE, PROF. SAMUEL, is mayor of the city of Albion, Mich., Secretary of the Board of Trustees of Albion College, and Chairman of the National Committee of the Prohibition Party. He was born in Oxford County, Canada, near Princeton, June 6th, 1851, and graduated from Albion College, June, 1872. For ten years he was Professor of Astronomy and Physics in Albion College, and has given special attention to Sunday School work.

DOHERTY, R. R., PH.D.

DOHERTY, ROBERT R., PH.D., is well known as one of the writers of Hurlburt and Doherty's Illustrated Notes on the Sunday School Lessons, and author of "The Torch-bearers of Christendom," one of the books of the Epworth League Reading Course, 1896-97. He was born December 24th, 1847. He served as one of the secretaries of the General Conference in 1888. He was the first Recording Secretary of the Epworth League, and is now Assistant Secretary of the Sunday School Union and Tract Society, also a member of the Board of Control.

DOTY, O. L., ESQ., is a successful business man in Cleveland, O. He was born at Pottsdam, New York, in 1856. For eight years he was President of the Cleveland District Epworth League North Ohio Conference, and for twelve years occupied the position of Superintendent of Jennings Avenue M. E. Sunday School. He is now President of the Fifth General Conference District Epworth League, which comprises the States of Ohio and Kentucky, and in addition thereto the Conferences of North China and South America. He has been a member of the Board of Control, and also of the General Cabinet. He was present at the formation of the Epworth League, and prior to its existence was State Secretary of the Ohio Oxford League.

DUNCAN, REV. W. W., is Bishop of the Methodist Episcopal Church South. He was born at Randolph, Va., December 20th, 1839, and educated at Randolph Macon College, and at Wofford College, South Carolina. Entered the ministry in 1858. He has been a regular pastor, professor in a church college, and was elected to the Presidency of Randolph Macon College, but declined, preferring to remain in the pastorate.

BISHOP DUNCAN.

DUBOSE, REV. HORACE M., is pastor of the First Methodist Episcopal Church South, Jackson, Miss. He was born on a cotton plantation in the State of Alabama, November 7th, 1858, and entered the ministry in 1876. He has been stationed at Galveston, Texas; Houston, Texas; Los Angeles, Cal.; Tyler, Texas. For one year he was editor of the Los Angeles *Christian Advocate*, and for four years served as connexional editor of the *Methodist Advocate*, San Francisco. While pastor of Trinity Church, Los Angeles, he organized a movement which resulted in the Epworth League of the Methodist Episcopal Church South.

EATON, REV. HOMER, D.D., is Senior Book Agent of the Methodis Book Concern, New York City. He is a native of New England, having been born in the State of Vermont, a little more than sixty years ago. He was converted in early youth and became an active member of the Methodist Episcopal Church. He took a theological course in the Methodist Biblical Institute at Concord, N. H. Has been secretary of his Conference, delegate to the General Conference, and one of the fraternal delegates to the General Conference of the Methodist Church in Canada. He was also delegate to the first Ecumenical Methodist Conference held in London, Eng., in 1881. In February, 1889, he was elected to his present position in place of John M. Philips.

REV. HOMER EATON, D.D.

EWERS, REV. M. H., of Tuscola, Illinois, was born in Marietta, Ohio, March 20, 1850. Reared to manhood in Wisconsin. Moved to Paris, Ill., at majority. Studied law. Practised law two years. Was converted at the age of thirty. Joined the Illinois Conference in 1882. Actively engaged in church work since. Was four years President of the Danville District Epworth League.

FLEMING, MR. R. J., is mayor of the city of Toronto, a position to which he has been elected four times. He is a member of Parliament Street Methodist Church. Mr. Fleming is a man of about thirty-seven years of age.

EDWARDS, REV. ARTHUR, A.M., D.D., is editor of the *Northwestern Christian Advocate*, Chicago. He was born at Norwalk, O., in 1834, and educated at Ohio Wesleyan University, Delaware, graduating in 1858. He held pastorates in the Detroit Conference until 1861, when he went into the army as first chaplain of the Michigan Infantry, and passed through a dozen historical battles. He came to Chicago in 1864 to become assistant editor of the *Northwestern*, serving as such under Dr. T. M. Eddy and Dr. J. M. Reid. In 1872 he was elected editor, and has held the position until now. He has served on the Epworth League Board of Control for four years, and has been a member of every General Conference since 1872.

REV. ARTHUR EDWARDS, A.M., D.D.

FOSS, REV. HERBERT E., A.M., was born in Wales, Maine, December 25th, 1857. In 1882 he joined the Maine Conference. In 1891 he was transferred to the East Maine Conference, and stationed at Grace Church, Bangor. After a pastorate of five years he was appointed to the First Church in the same city, where he now is. For four years he has been President of the East Maine Conference League, and a member of the Cabinet of the First General Conference District League. Mr. Foss has been closely identified with the young people's movement from the beginning, preaching, lecturing and attending conventions and mass meetings in many parts of New England.

FULLER, MR. F. D., is a lawyer residing in Topeka, Kansas. He is a member of the First M. E. Church. Was born in the State of Maine, 1862, and educated at the Wesleyan University, Middleton, Conn., and Boston University. Has been a member of the Board of Control of the Epworth League of the M. E. Church since 1891.

FITZGERALD, REV. O. P., is Bishop of the Methodist Episcopal Church South, and resides at Nashville, Tenn. He was born in Caswell County, N.C., August 24th, 1829, and was educated in the County schools, ending with "Oak Grove Academy," somewhat famous in its day. Entered the ministry in 1853. Bishop Fitzgerald was a missionary in the mines of California in the early days. He has been editor of the *Pacific Methodist*, the *Christian Spectator*, the *California Teacher*, and the *Christian Advocate*, the official organ of the M. E. Church South, for four years. He was Superintendent of Public Instruction for the State of California for four years. At the General Conference held at St. Louis in May, 1890, he was elected to the office of Bishop. He has been the author of a number of valuable books, among which may be mentioned, "Christian Growth," "California Sketches," "The Life of McFerrin," "Eminent Methodists," and "The Epworth League Book." Some of these have had a very large sale. A large part of the Bishop's life has been devoted to editorial work, and he has always taken a very great interest in the work of the Epworth League.

BISHOP O. P. FITZGERALD.

FRASER, REV. B. F., is pastor of the M. E. Church South at Alberton, Ga. He was born in Georgia, 1860, and educated at Emory College, Oxford, Ga. He has been stationed at Toccoa, Cave Spring, Rome, Augusta, Dalton, all in the North Georgia Conference.

GARY, REV. FRANK, is pastor of the M. E. Church at Galveston, Tex. He is a member of the Board of Control of the Epworth League of the M. E. Church, and has been secretary of the Texas Conference. Has twice declined the presiding eldership. Mr. Gary was born in South Carolina in 1862, and educated at Wylie University, Marshall, took a theological course at Gammon Theological Seminary, Atlanta, Ga.

FLAVELLE, MR. J. W., is General Treasurer of the Epworth League in Canada. He is Managing Director of the Davies Pork Packing Co., of Toronto, and Sunday School Superintendent of Sherbourne Street Church.

J. W. FLAVELLE, ESQ.

FOSTER, MRS. MARY, is the wife of the Rev. Wm. W. Foster, of Troy, New York Conference; she is a member of the American Authors' Guild, and a well-known writer of books and magazine articles; she prepares the Kindergarten notices for the *Teacher's Journal*, and is a Kindergarten trainer of wide reputation; she is the author of the Junior Hymnal used largely by Junior Epworth Leagues, but is perhaps better known by her valuable work, "The Kindergarten of the Church." The training of children according to the principles of the New Education is a specialty with Mrs. Foster, and she has been the Chautauqua lecturer for two years past on this subject. She has done much to open the way for the adoption of improved methods of impressing the youngest children with the fundamental ideas of religion and the first facts of Christianity. Mrs. Foster's address is 150 Fifth Ave., New York City.

GRIFFITH, REV. THOS., PH.D., is pastor of the Wall Street Methodist Church, Brockville, Ont. He was born in the county of Frontenac, Ontario, 1844, and entered the ministry in 1864. He took a three years' course in the University of Toronto, which in later years was followed by a course in philosophy at Bloomington, Ill. Dr. Griffith was a member of the Committee that formulated the basis of union for the federation of the Methodisms of Canada, and President of the Montreal Conference at the consummation of the Union. He has also been Secretary of the Toronto Conference and Assistant Secretary of the General Conference. Last year he had the honor of being President of the Montreal Conference Epworth League.

GERMAN, MR. C. E., is general agent of the Ontario Mutual Life Assurance Company, and resides at Strathroy, Ont. He is a member of the Front Street Methodist Church. For some years Mr. German has been Superintendent of the Sunday School, and was also President of the Middlesex County Sunday School Association.

FOWLER, REV. CHAS. H., D.D., LL.D., is Bishop of the Methodist Episcopal Church. He was born in Burford, Ont., Canada, August 11th, 1837. He made his way with little aid through both College and the Theological School, living part of the time on but a few cents a week; walking across the country, carrying his valise on his back, to save stage fare, and during the summer vacation working as a farm hand. During the vacations in his theology course he taught school. At the end of eight years' hard work he was but $13 in debt. He was an accomplished swimmer, and while studying at the Garrett Biblical Institute performed heroic feats by rescuing passengers from the wreck of the *Lady Elgin*. As a student, he was especially able as a mathematician and orator. In 1858 he commenced the study of law in Chicago, but before being admitted to the bar he yielded to the convictions of his early years and gave himself to the ministry. The eleven years of his pastorate were spent in Chicago. From 1872 to 1876 he was President of the Northwestern University. In 1876 the General Conference elected him to the editorship of the New York *Christian Advocate*, which position he held until 1880, when he was chosen General Missionary Secretary. Under his administration the income of the Missionary Society greatly increased. In May, 1884, he was elected Bishop by the General Conference in Philadelphia. He was ordained by Bishop Simpson, this being the last official act of that eminent divine. Bishop Fowler resides in Minneapolis.

BISHOP FOWLER.

HACKNEY, MR. GEO. L., is editor of the *Epworth News*, Asheville, N.C., which has a circulation of 1,500, and is the only Epworth League paper published in the State. He was born in Yorkshire, England, sixteen miles from Epworth, the birthplace of Wesley. He has been President of Asheville District Epworth League Conference, and a member of the Epworth League Board of the Western North Carolina Conference, M. E. Church South. He is now a member of the Central M. E. Church South, Asheville, N.C.

HAMILTON, REV. J. W., D.D., is corresponding secretary of the Freedman's Aid and Southern Education Society, with headquarters in Cincinnati. He was born in the State of Virginia in 1845, and graduated at Mount Union College, Ohio. United with the Pittsburg Conference in 1866, was transferred to the New England Conference in 1868, and stationed in Boston for twenty years. Dr. Hamilton was the founder, and pastor for nine years, of the People's Church in that city. He has written several books, among which may be mentioned "The People's Church Pulpit," and "Lives of Methodist Bishops."

REV. J. W. HAMILTON, D.D.

HAMMOND, REV. J. D., is president of the Wesleyan College for Women, Macon, Ga., and is connected with the M. E. Church South. He was educated in the University of Georgia, and in Drew Theological Seminary. Has been pastor for twelve years, and president of Central College, Fayette, eight years. Assumed his present position last September.

HAMNER, REV. W. F., is pastor of the Central M. E. Church South, Memphis, Tenn. Was born in Tennessee, 1858, and educated in the University of Mississippi. Before entering the ministry he spent four years in the practice of law. He has been pastor in Brunswick, Dyersburg, Tenn., Roanoke, Va., Baltimore, Md.

HARD, REV. MANLY S., D.D., is assistant corresponding secretary of the Board of Church Extension of the Methodist Episcopal Church, and resides in Kingston, Pa. He was born at Pennfield, N.Y., in 1842, and graduated at Syracuse University. Has been pastor in Clinton, Ilion, Syracuse, Ithaca, Canadaigua and Binghamton. Has also been presiding elder and a trustee of Ezra Cornell Library, Wyoming Conference Seminary. Was assistant secretary of the General Conference in 1884, '88, '92 and '96.

REV. MANLY S. HARD, D.D.

HARRISON, REV. J. E., B.A., is a native of Tennessee. He was educated at Webb School and Vanderbilt University, where he was a tutor for a short time. After ten years in the pastorate in charge of important stations, he became in 1894 President of San Antonio Female College, San Antonio, Texas, a Methodist college for the higher education of young ladies. He has written a book on the Epworth League, entitled "Our New Building."

HAMSHER, MISS LIBBIE R., is superintendent of the Junior Leagues in the State of Illinois, and is connected with the First M. E. Church, Monmouth, Ill. She has given special attention to Junior work, and has compiled and arranged a Junior hand-book or manual for the work and workers of Illinois.

HATHORNE, MISS FLORENCE, of Chicago, Ill., has given her life to the mission work of that great city. Educated in the Chicago Public Schools she began her work in the Chicago Newsboys' Home, leaving which she took charge of a school in the Chicago Waifs' Mission. For four years she has been in charge of the daily school in Cook County Jail, during which time she has come into contact with two thousand of Chicago's youthful criminals.

HARDY, HON. A. S., Q.C., M.P.P., was born at Mount Pleasant, Brant County, Ont., 14th December, 1837. Commenced to practise law in 1865, in Brantford, when he rapidly rose to prominence. In 1873 he accepted the nomination for South Brant as candidate for the Ontario Legislature, and has represented that riding continuously either by acclamation or by increased majorities ever since. In 1877 he became a member of Mr. Mowat's Government as Provincial Secretary. In 1889 he assumed the Commissionership of Crown Lands, and about a year ago be became Premier of Ontario and Attorney-General. As a legislator he has shown great energy and ability. He is also a very effective speaker.

HON. A. S. HARDY.

HART, MR. G. N., was brought up on the farm, attended college, and afterwards became a travelling salesman. He is now in business in Pine Bluff, Ark., and is connected with the Methodist Episcopal Church South.

HAVEN, REV. W. I., D.D., is pastor of St. Mark's M. E. Church, Brookline, Mass. He was born at Westfield, Mass., January 30th, 1856, and educated at the Wesleyan University at Middletown, Conn., Drew Theological Seminary and Boston University. He entered the ministry in 1881, and most of his pastorates have been in and about Boston. He has occupied several positions in Epworth League organizations.

HUESTIS, REV. CHAS. H., was born at Jacksonville, N.B., 1863, and educated at Mount Allison Academy and University, taking the degree of B.A., in 1885. Was ordained in 1888. Has been stationed at Weymouth, Hebron, Port Hood, Bridgewater, Bermuda and Barrington, all in the Nova Scotia Conference.

HASTINGS, GENERAL DANIEL H., Governor of Pennsylvania, was born in Clinton County, February 26th, 1849. He was the youngest of five sons, and went to work at an early age. At fourteen he was doing a man's work on the farm. At the common schools of the neighborhood he acquired all the learning they could furnish, and in 1863, before he was fifteen years old, learning of a school that had no teacher, he walked twenty miles through the snow, was examined, and got the position. He made his mark as a teacher, and in 1867 came to Bellefonte as principal of the Academy. Choosing law as his profession, he was admitted to the bar in 1875. He practised until 1888, when he gave up his profession and associated himself with ex-Governor James A. Beaver, and others, in the development of coal fields. At the time of the Johnstown flood, General Hastings was placed in charge of the relief operations, and his work was given freely, unwearyingly, and without pay or reward. Named after one of its faithful itinerant ministers, Governor Hastings entered the Methodist Episcopal Church in boyhood, and has been for twenty years a trustee of the Bellefonte congregation. He is a member of the General Church Extension Board of the Methodist Episcopal Church, and a trustee of Dickinson College, Carlisle. As an orator his services are in great demand, and many of his addresses have attracted marked attention by their eloquence and breadth of thought.

GOVERNOR HASTINGS.

HILL, REV. JAMES, was born in Texas, 1854, and entered the ministry in his twenty-first year; served one year as State Secretary of the Epworth League and two years as associate editor of the Texas *Christian Advocate*. He is now pastor of the Denton Street Church, Gainesville, Texas, one of the finest churches of the State. He is the author of two books, "North Texas Pulpit," and "Texas Characters," and is President of the Texas Authors' Association.

HENDERSON, REV. JAMES, D.D., is Assistant Secretary of the Missionary Society of the Methodist Church, Canada. He was brought up in the Presbyterian faith and received his education in Glasgow. Coming to Canada he entered the ministry of the Methodist Church and was ordained in 1876. He has been stationed at Sherbrooke, Cookshire, Huntingdon, Prescott and Montreal. In the latter city he filled three different pastorates, Dominion Square, Sherbrooke Street and St. James'. In Toronto Dr. Henderson has been pastor of Carlton Street and Sherbourne Street churches. One year ago he was taken from the pulpit of the latter church and elected to his present position. He travels throughout the Dominion attending missionary anniversaries.

REV. JAS. HENDERSON, D.D.

HOUCK, REV. D. S., is pastor of the Main Street Methodist Church, Picton, Ont. He was born in 1861 in Ontario, Can., and educated at Victoria University. One of the first Epworth League District organizations in Ontario was effected chiefly through his efforts, and he was elected as first president. He is now First Vice-President of the Bay of Quinte Conference Epworth League, and also President of the Inter-denominational Union for the District. He has always taken an active part in Epworth League work.

JONES, REV. CHAS. O., A.M., is pastor of the Centenary M. E. Church South, Chattanooga. He was born in North Carolina and is now in his forty-eighth year. He is an honor graduate of Emory College, Oxford, Ga.; has been stationed in St. Louis, Kansas City, Dallas, Tex., and Louisville, Ky. Mr. Jones has written much for the secular and religious press. He was for four years editor of the Sunday School department of the *Southwestern Methodist*, and for two years in charge of the same work in the Texas *Christian Advocate*; has been editor of the devotional department of the *Epworth Era* from the beginning.

JORDON, REV. W. H., A.M., is pastor of the First M. E. Church, Sioux Falls, S.D. Was born in the State of Massachusetts in 1857, and educated at Northwestern University, Evanston, Ill. His father was a Methodist minister, a member of the New England ¡Conference. Mr. Jordon has spent some time as a teacher, has been presiding elder and was reserve delegate to the General Conference of 1892. At present he is a member of the Board of Control of the M. E. Church.

HENDRIX, REV. E. R., D.D., is Bishop of the M. E. Church South.

BISHOP HENDRIX.

He was born in the State of Missouri in 1847, graduated at Wesleyan University, Middleton, and Union Theological Seminary, New York City. Entered the ministry in 1869. Was a pastor for nine years, President of Central College eight years, and has been Bishop for eleven years. Bishop Hendrix is much interested in missionary and educational work among Leaguers. After his visit to Korea in 1895 he enlisted the Epworth Leagues to support two missionary families in Korea. He has also given much attention to similar work among the Leaguers in Texas who support several missionaries in China and Mexico. Bishop Hendrix resides at Kansas City, Mo.

KEENEY, REV. F. T., is pastor of the Hedding M. E. Church, Elmira, N.Y. Was born in New York State in 1863, educated at Syracuse University, and entered the ministry in 1886. He has contributed articles to the religious press for a number of years, and is frequently called on for addresses in Epworth League and Sunday School work.

KELLEY, REV. D. C., D.D., is a native Tennessean. He graduated from Cumberland University, Lebanon, Tenn. He spent 1852 and 1853 in China, but was forced on account of the ill-health of his wife to return to America. He has filled as a pastor the foremost charges in his

Conference; spent seven years as pastor of McKendree Church, Nashville, the leading Church in Southern Methodism. The plan to establish Central University which resulted finally, through Commodore Vanderbilt's generosity, in Vanderbilt University, was inaugurated by Dr. Kelley—as was the scheme to relieve the indebtedness of the Southern Methodist Publishing House when at the point of bankruptcy in 1878. He was the first promoter of the organization of the Woman's Board of Foreign Missions in Southern Methodism, and was for some years President of the State Humane Society.

HURST, REV. JOHN F., D.D., is Bishop of the Methodist Episcopal Church, and Chancellor of the American University. He was born near Salem, Md., August 17th, 1834, educated at Dickinson College, Carlisle, Pa., and in the Universities of Halle and Heidelberg, Germany. He entered the ministry in 1858, occupying pastorates for eight years in New Jersey, Staten Island. He was Professor of Theology in the Mission Institute, Bremen, Germany, from 1866 to 1869, and in Martin Mission Institute, Frankfort, from 1869 to 1871. He then became Professor of Historical Theology in Drew Theological College, Madison, N.J., and after nine years was elected President, which position he occupied for eight years, when he was elected Bishop in 1880. His residence is in Washington, D.C. During recent years Bishop Hurst has given special attention to the American University, the interests of which he has greatly promoted through the press and on the platform.

BISHOP HURST.

KELLY, MR. R. M., is Secretary and Treasurer of the Longview Kelly Plow Manufacturing Company, Texas. He is connected with the Methodist Episcopal Church South, and is President of the East Texas Conference Epworth League.

JOHNSON, REV. SIMPSON, is the representative of the Wesley Guild, and resides at Manchester, Eng. He is forty-four years of age, and was born at Barnard Castle, on the border line between Yorkshire and Durham, which has been immortalized by Sir Walter Scott, in "Rokeby." Mr. Johnson was converted in early youth, and began to preach at seventeen. Was appointed by the Conference to his first circuit before he was twenty-one years of age. All through his ministry he has been specially interested in young people, and has been the means of taking by the hand many a friendless young man and putting him on the pathway to success. He is Financial Secretary of his district, Secretary of the Examining Board for candidates for the ministry, and is one of the secretaries of the Wesley Guild, having sole charge of the Bible and Prayer Union Department. One who knows him well says " he is a splendid speaker, and his fame is in every home in the north-west of England. His annual visits are looked forward to with increasing interest from year to year." He has filled some of the most important pulpits, being stationed at Bishop Auckland, Hull, Liverpool, London and Manchester.

REV. SIMPSON JOHNSON.

KERBY, REV. G. W., B.A., was born July 18th, 1860, and graduated from Victoria College in 1888. At present he is pastor of the Welland Avenue Church, St. Catharines, and invited to the pastorate of Brant Avenue Church, Brantford. Mr. Kerby is President of the Hamilton Conference Epworth League, and is the originator of the " Forward Movement in Evangelistic Work and Bible Study." He is a member of the General Board of the Epworth League. He is gifted as a singer as well as a preacher.

KETCHAM, REV. HEBER D., was born at Kenton, Ohio, December 29th, 1859, graduating from the Ohio Wesleyan University in 1881; was admitted to the Cincinnati Conference in 1884, and has been stationed at Mount Washington, Wilmington, Cincinnati and Hillsborough. He has occupied the position of President and Secretary of the Cincinnati Conference League, also that of President and First Vice-President of the fifth General Conference League.

KIMBALL, REV. CLARENCE O., was born August 23rd, 1868, at Golconda, Ill., U.S.A., educated in the Public schools of his native place, and later at Austin College, where he received his A.B. Earned his A.M. and Ph.D. degrees by graduate work at McKendree College, Lebanon, Ill. Had valuable training in practical business, where his experience in winning his way was varied. Learned the printer's trade and became a country editor, taught school, served as a court clerk. Admitted to the bar in 1889 and practised his profession. Entered the ministry, January, 1894. Is now pastor of the M. E. Church at St. Elmo, in the Southern Illinois Conference.

KNOTT, REV. J. O., is pastor of the Epworth Church, Washington, D.C., and is connected with the M. E. Church South. He was born near Harper's Ferry in 1859. When eighteen years of age he taught school, afterwards going to Vanderbilt University, Nashville, where he graduated in 1883. Has been stationed at Arlington, near Baltimore, Frederick City, Md., and two churches in West Virginia. Has travelled extensively in the Old Land.

KYNETT, REV. A. J., D.D., LL.D., is Secretary of the Board of Church Extension of the Methodist Episcopal Church, residing in Philadelphia, Pa. He is one of the chief promoters of the Anti-Saloon League of America, and is prominently identified with the temperance movement in Pennsylvania. He is to speak on the Anti-Saloon League of America on Saturday evening.

LANCELEY, REV. JOHN E., is pastor of Grace Methodist Church, Brampton. He was born in England in 1848, and received his education at Victoria College, Cobourg. He has been stationed at Chatham, Guelph, Niagara Falls, London, St. Thomas, Thorold, Toronto and Barrie. He is at present Chairman of the Brampton District and a member of the General Epworth League Board for the Dominion. Mr. Lanceley was invited to the pastorate of Mount Vernon Place M. E. Church, Baltimore, Md., in 1893, but was not admitted into the Baltimore Conference. He is the author of a book of sermons, and a writer for several papers and magazines. He is also widely known on the lecture platform.

LAZIER, MISS FLORENCE, was born at Shannonville, Ont., and educated at the Ontario Ladies' College, Whitby. For several years she has occupied the position of permanent Secretary of the Epworth League in the Bridge Street Methodist Church, Belleville, Can. This office involves, not only the usual work of a secretary, such as correspondence, etc., but the supervision of a free reading room and parlors which are kept open every afternoon and evening of the week, with the exception of Sunday.

LEACH, REV. WILLIAM B., D.D., is pastor of St. Paul's Church, Chicago. He was born near Millbank, Ont., in 1852, and removed to Illinois in 1864, joined the Rock River Conference in 1879, and was educated at the Northwestern University, Evanston, Ill., taking the degrees of B.A., B.D., and Ph.D. The honorary degree of D.D. was conferred upon him by Murphy College, Tennessee. In his preaching, Dr. Leach has given great prominence to Christian citizenship, and he has also paid great attention to Sunday School work. He has many calls to lecture, but devotes his best efforts to his pastorate.

LEY, REV. J. B., is pastor of the Trinity M. E. Church South, Tallahassee, Fla. He was born in Georgia, 1855, but reared in Florida; converted when nineteen years of age, and entered the ministry in his twenty-first year. He is a member of the Board of Trustees Wesleyan Female College at Macon, and Chaplain of the State Seminary.

MACLAREN, J. J., Q.C., LL.D., was born in the Province of Quebec, 1842, and educated at Victoria College, Cobourg. Studied law in McGill University, Montreal. Dr. Maclaren is a trustee, local preacher and Bible-class teacher in the Metropolitan Church, Toronto; President of the Provincial Sunday School Association for Ontario, Representative of Ontario on the International Sunday School Committee, Director and Trustee of the Y.M.C.A., Member of the Board of Regents, Victoria University; member of the Senate of Toronto University, Counsel for the Methodist Church of the Dominion, Member of the General Board of Missions of the Methodist Church, and of the General Conference Special Committee and of the Church Court of Appeal. He was Canadian delegate at the Methodist Ecumenical Conference at Washington, 1891.

MAGEE, MR. CHARLES R., is manager of the New England Methodist Book Depository, Boston. Was born in New York State, 1851, and has lived in Boston nearly all his life. Entered the Methodist Book Concern in 1869 as a clerk, and succeeded to its management on the death of his father in 1888. He is a member of the Centre M. E. Church, Malden, Secretary of the Board of Trustees and Recording Steward. He is also Secretary of the Boston Wesleyan Association which publishes *Zion's Herald*, and is President of the Methodist Social Union. Mr. Magee is a member of the Board of Control for the First General Conference District.

MAHOOD, REV. J. W., is a Canadian, having been born in Huron County, Ont., in 1864. He was for three years a probationer in the Guelph

Conference, serving on the Fordwich and Dundalk circuits, and in 1887 was received into the Northwest Iowa Conference on credentials. He is at present pastor of the First Methodist Episcopal Church in Webster City, and is Vice-President for the Iowa Christian Citizenship League, and Chairman of the Iowa State Epworth League Assembly Commission. He is joint author of the "Young People's History of Methodism," published by the Methodist Book Concern; also the author of a little booklet on League work, entitled "The Missing Wheel Found."

MASON, REV. M. C. B., is Corresponding Secretary of the Freedman's Aid and Southern Education Society. Was born in Louisville, Ky., March 17th, 1859. Educated at New Orleans University and Gammon Theological Seminary, Ga. Previous to his present appointment he spent nine years in the pastorate. He has given special attention to the Mercy and Help Department of the League, and to temperance and prohibition.

MASSEY, MR. W. E. H., is President of the Massey-Harris Manufacturing Company, Toronto, Ont., and an official member of the Central Methodist Church, Toronto. He was born at Newcastle, Ont., in 1864, and educated at the Brookes' Military Academy, Cleveland, and Boston University, Boston, Mass. Mr. Massey has given special attention to Sunday School work, particularly with young men. For some years he has been a member of the Missionary Executive Committee of the Methodist Church, as well as a director of several of the charitable, religious and educational institutions of the city.

MELEAR, REV. J. M., A.B., D.D., is pastor of the First M. E. Church, Athens, Tenn., which has one of the most flourishing leagues in the Conference. He was born in Tennessee, 1868. Received his degrees from the Grant University, Chattanooga, being valedictorian of his class. He joined the Holston Conference in 1892.

MITCHELL, REV. CHAS. B., D.D., is pastor of the Hennepin Avenue Methodist Episcopal Church, Minneapolis. He was born in Alleghany City, Pa., Aug. 27th, 1857, and educated at Alleghany College, Meadville, Pa., from which institution he received the degrees of A.B., D.D. and Ph.D. During his ministry he has occupied prominent positions at Leavenworth, Kansas, Pittsburg, Plainfield (N.J.), Kansas City and Minneapolis. He has always been a pastor, having refused two invitations to become a college president. In League work he has made a specialty of conducting in his own church a Sunday night League after-meeting. In Kansas City there were over fifteen hundred conversions at these services in five winters. Dr. Mitchell has travelled extensively in Europe and Palestine. He has published a volume of travels, entitled "Gleaned from Three Continents."

MONK, REV. ALONSO, D.D., is a man of forty-three years of age; has been stationed at Little Rock, Camden, Tuscaloosa, Anniston, Ala., Memphis, Tenn., and is now in his fourth year as pastor of the Mulberry Street M. E. Church South, Macon., Ga., an old historical church with a membership of about one thousand. Dr. Monk has taken special interest in the Epworth League ever since its inception, and has always had a flourishing League.

MOORE, REV. DAVID H., D.D., LL.D., editor of the *Western Christian Advocate*, was born at Athens, O. Educated at Ohio University, and entered the ministry in 1860. He was captain, major, and lieutenant-colonel in the army, and has occupied the best of pastorates.

REV. D. H. MOORE, D.D.

MOORE, REV. T. ALBERT, is pastor of the Methodist Church, Palmerston, Ont., and chairman of the Palmerston District. He was born at Acton in 1860. Before entering the ministry he was in the newspaper business, on the staff of the Acton *Free Press*. He has been stationed at Drumbo, Princeton, Hamilton, Niagara Falls, and Dunnville. Mr. Moore has given special attention to the Junior work of the League. He was the first superintendent of Junior Epworth Leagues in Canadian Methodism, and is at present Vice-President of the Junior Department of the Hamilton Conference League.

MORSE, REV. S. A., is a son of Abishai Morse, who was a local preacher of the Methodist Church in Canada for a number of years. Mr. Morse was associate editor of the Buffalo *Christian Advocate*, and afterwards editor. He was a member of the General Conference of 1896, and is now a member of the General Board of Control of the Epworth League of the Methodist Episcopal Church. He has written much for the *Epworth Herald*, and other papers, in the interest of the League.

MURLIN, REV. L. H., A.B., S.T.B., President of Baker University, Baldwin, Kansas. He was born November 16th, 1861, in Mercer County, Ohio, and graduated from Fort Wayne College, Indiana, in 1886; has been a pastor at Knightsville, and Vincennes, Ind. In 1894 he was appointed to his present position. He is a member of the American Institute of Christian Philosophy.

MURRAH, REV. WM. P., D D., is President of Millsaps College, Jacksonville, Miss. Dr. Murrah was born in Alabama in 1851. He graduated at the Southern University, Greensboro', in 1874, and has given very much attention to educational matters. He is a member of the North Mississippi Conference of the M. E. Church South. As a pastor he filled some of the most important stations within the bounds of his Conference. By appointment of the bishops of his Church, he was a delegate to the Ecumenical Conference, which met in Washington in 1891.

MURRAY, REV. JAS. C., D.D., is a member of the faculty of Gammon Theological Seminary, Atlanta, Ga., an institution for the education of colored people. He was born in the State of Indiana, July 19th, 1848, and educated in the National Normal University, Lebanon, Ohio, and in Drew Theological Seminary. He began teaching in the public schools when a mere boy, and spent fourteen years as teacher previous to entering the ministry. The special work to which Dr. Murray has given attention is the effort to popularize the study of the English Bible. To further this end he has given lectures, prepared outline studies, held institutes, and published text-books for students' use.

McDOWELL, REV. W. F., B.A., is Chancellor of the University at Denver, Col., and is a member of the State Board of Charities and Corrections for the State. He was born in Millersboro', O., February, 1858. He took the degree of B.A. in the Ohio University in 1879, and graduated with the degree of S.T.B. in Boston University. Entered the ministry in 1872, North Ohio Conference.

McMURRAY, REV. W. F., was born in the State of Missouri, 1864, was educated at St. Charles College, and at Central College, Missouri, and entered the ministry in 1886. He is now a pastor of the M. E. Church South at Richmond, Mo. He has been pastor at St. Joseph, Macon and Richmond, Mo. At present he is agent for Central College, a school for the higher education of girls and young women. He is also President of the Missouri State Epworth League.

NAFTZGER, REV. L. J., is pastor of High Street Church, Muncie, Ind., which has a membership of nearly thirteen hundred, and is one of the most important churches in the State. He is Secretary of his Conference, and is President of the Island Park Assembly Association, the oldest Western Chautauqua. He has always been greatly interested in the work of the Epworth League, paying special attention to the Mercy and Help and Spiritual Work departments.

NEWMAN, REV. J. P., D.D., LL.D., is Bishop of the Methodist Episcopal Church, residing in New York City. He was elected to his high office in 1888. He was three times pastor of the Metropolitan Church, Washington, the pulpit of which is now occupied by Rev. Hugh Johnston, D.D. He was the particular friend of General Grant, who attended his congregation. The Bishop is remarkable for many things. He has a fine presence, attractive delivery, and a splendid voice. His insight into the Scriptures is said to be marvellous, and his preaching is exceedingly edifying, as well as entertaining. He will deliver his popular lecture, entitled "Around the Footstool," in Cooke's Church on Thursday evening, July 15th. It will probably be a cause for regret to many that they will not be able to hear both Bishop Newman and Bishop Fowler ; but a selection will have to be made, as they are to speak at the same hour.

BISHOP NEWMAN.

NEWMAN, REV. J. W., D.D., is presiding elder of the Birmingham District M. E. Church South, and resides at Birmingham, Ala. Was born in the State of Alabama, 1846, and educated in Union Academy and Willsville Institute. He is 2nd Vice-President of the Epworth League Board of the M. E. Church South, and President of the Alabama State League. Was elected editor of the Alabama *Christian Advocate* in 1891, but declined to serve.

NINDE, REV. ED. S., is pastor of the Tabernacle Church, Detroit, and son of Bishop Ninde. Was born in Cincinnati, O., in 1866, graduated from Wesleyan University in 1887, spent two years in Europe, taking a post-graduate course in the University at Berlin. He entered the Detroit Conference in 1891.

NORMAN, REV. D., B.A., is a probationer in the Methodist Church, Canada, attending Victoria University. He is one of the most active workers in "The Students' Missionary Campaign."

McCABE, BISHOP C. C., was born in Ohio sixty years ago. He preached in that State till the war broke out, and then enlisted as chaplain of the 122nd Ohio Volunteers, in which regiment nearly all the young men in his congregation enlisted. He "had to go to look after the boys," as he said, and it was because of his untiring devotion to their needs, bodily as well as spiritual, on the battlefield and in the hospital, that the title of "Chaplain" has followed him ever since the war. He was taken prisoner after the battle at Winchester while remaining behind to care for the wounded and bury the dead, and was taken to Libby Prison, where he was kept for four months. After his release he devoted himself to raising money for the Christian Commission, and turned many thousands of dollars into the treasury for the relief of the soldiers. For several years he was Missionary Secretary of the M. E. Church, and travelled all over the continent, kindling missionary enthusiasm everywhere.

BISHOP M'CABE.

NYE, REV. C. L., was born in Dudley, Mass., in 1854; came to Iowa in 1876, and joined the Des Moines Conference, where he has spent all his ministry. He was President of the Iowa State Epworth League at its organization, and has edited the League department in the Inland and Omaha *Christian Advocate* for the last seven years. He is now pastor at Perry, Ia., one of the best churches in the Conference, with a membership of about five hundred.

ODELL, REV. WILLIS P., D.D., was born in Laconia, N.H., December 14th, 1855. Took his collegiate and theological course in Boston University, where he was granted the degrees of A.B., A.M., and Ph.D. His degree of D.D. was given by Alleghany College in 1885. His appointments have been Cliftondale, Salem, Malden, Mass., Delaware Avenue, and Richmond Avenue, Buffalo. He is now pastor of the latter church, which has seven hundred members and one thousand Sunday School scholars. Dr. Odell was one of the twenty-seven original organizers of the Epworth League.

NINDE, BISHOP WILLIAM XAVIER, D.D., LL.D., was born June 21, 1832, in Cordlandville, N.Y., consequently he is now in his sixty-fifth year. He graduated from Wesleyan University in 1855, where his scholarship was of high rank. After graduation he taught a year, and then joined the Black River Conference, and served several churches with increasing acceptability. In 1861 he was transferred to the Cincinnati Conference, and for some eight years was successively pastor of several of the principal churches in that city. He spent a year or two travelling in Europe and the East. On his return, in 1870, he was transferred to the Detroit Conference, and stationed at the Central Church in Detroit. At the close of this pastorate he was elected to the chair of Practical Theology in Garrett Biblical Institute at Evanston, Ill., of which institution he became president in 1879. He was elected Bishop in 1884, and is now President of the Epworth League in the Methodist Episcopal Church.

BISHOP NINDE.

ORR, REV. JOHN C., was born in the State of Virginia, in 1858, and educated at Vanderbilt University. He joined the Holston Conference in the autumn of 1886. He has been stationed at Woznesville, N.C., Chattanooga, Tenn., Prelaski, Va., Morristown, Tenn., and is now pastor of the M. E. Church South, at Cleveland, Tenn. He is President of the Holston Conference Epworth League, and is gifted as a singer.

OSBON, REV. E. S., D.D., is presiding elder of the New York District of the New York Annual Conference, and lives at Yonkers. He is a member of the Board of Control of the Epworth League from the General Conference District, and was also a member of the original Board of Control, when the League was founded. He was born at Middleboro', and graduated from Syracuse University.

PALMER, REV. ABRAHAM J., D.D., is Corresponding Secretary of the Missionary Society of the Methodist Episcopal Church. He was born in the State of New Jersey in 1847, enlisted in the war as a private soldier, Company "D," 48th Regiment New York State Volunteers, in 1861, when he was fourteen years old. It is supposed that he has the record of being the youngest enlisted soldier in the army that fought for the Union. He was captured in the deathly night assault at Fort Wagner, S.C., on the 18th of July, 1863, and confined for nine months in Confederate prison. He subsequently graduated from Western Middletown College, Connecticut, in 1870. Has been stationed at Grace Church, Staten Island; Waverley Church, Jersey City; Park Avenue and St. Paul's (second term), New York, and First Church, Yonkers, N.Y. New churches at Park Avenue, St. Paul's and Yonkers were built during his pastorate. In addition to a wide reputation as a preacher, he is well known throughout the country as a lecturer. His lecture, entitled "Company 'D,' the Die-no-mores," has been delivered many times. He received the degree of D.D. from Syracuse University and Alleghany College both on the same day, 1885.

REV. A. J. PALMER, D.D.

OXLEY, MR. J. McDONALD, B.A., LL.B., was born in Halifax in 1855, educated at Dalhousie College and Harvard University. Admitted to the Nova Scotia bar in 1878, and entered the civil service at Ottawa in 1882. At present he is Manager of the Montreal District for the Sun Life Assurance Co. Mr. Oxley has given much attention to journalism and literary work since 1878. He has published fifteen books and hundreds of short stories, sketches and articles, having contributed to over sixty of the English and American periodicals. His books are especially adapted for young people, and have been brought out by the best publishers of London, Edinburgh, New York, Boston and Philadelphia. He is an official member of St. James Methodist Church, Montreal, and gives special attention to the Literary department of the Epworth League.

PALMORE, REV. W. B., D.D., is editor of the St. Louis *Christian Advocate*. He was born in Tennessee and educated at Vanderbilt University, entered the ministry of the M. E. Church South in 1877, and was stationed in various cities. Has been Chaplain of the State Senate, and has travelled all over the world.

REV. W. B. PALMORE, D.D.

PARKER, REV. Z. A., D.D., is President of the Athens Female college, the second oldest college for women in the world. He was born in the State of Tennessee, 1851, educated at Emory and Henry College, Virginia, and Florence Wesleyan University. Has been presiding elder for eight years, and District Superintendent for the American Bible Society in Alabama and Florida. Has organized a large number of Epworth Leagues. Dr. Parker is connected with the M. E. Church South.

PARR, REV. WM. D., of Kokomo, Ind., was born in Indiana, 1854, and educated for the ministry at Drew Theological Seminary in 1878. Has been pastor in the North Indiana Conference since 1878, having spent the full legal term in five pastorates. During this time he has built four splendid churches. Mr. Parr is a member of the Epworth League Board of Control, and was a delegate to the last General Conference.

PARR, REV. T. J., B.A., is pastor of the Methodist Church, Merritton, Ont. He was born in Woodstock, Ont., and graduated from Toronto University with honors. He has given much study to the subject of elocution, and is a graduate of the Philadelphia School of Oratory. In Epworth League work he has taken an active part, holding various official positions, and is now one of the vice-presidents of the Hamilton Conference League. Mr. Parr writes the expositions of the Epworth League topics for the *Christian Guardian*, the official organ of the Methodist Church in Canada.

PATE, REV. J. T., D.D., was born in Sumter, B.C., June 27th, 1856. He was educated in the schools of his native town and at Wofford College. He has travelled extensively in the United States, Canada, and Europe. At the Pan-American Congress, held in Toronto, he was one of the leading speakers. At present he is pastor of the M. E. Church South, Camden, S.C.

PAYNE, REV. CHAS. H., LL.D., Secretary of the Board of Education of the Methodist Episcopal Church. He was born at Taunton, Mass., and educated at Providence Seminary, Wesleyan University, and Boston University School of Theology. Besides contributing largely to the secular and religious press he has published several books, the best known of which is probably "Guides and Guards in Character Building." He has lectured on "The Bible and the Nineteenth Century," and "The Epworth League and the Twentieth Century." For twelve years Dr. Payne was president of the Ohio Wesleyan University.

REV. C. H. PAYNE, LL.D.

PAYNE, B. L., M.D., is a graduate of the Ohio Medical College, and is practising in Lincoln, Neb. He is a member of St. Paul's M. E. Church, and is also a member of the Epworth League Board of Control. He is president of his local chapter and superintendent of the Sunday School. Dr. Payne has given much attention to the subject of church finances, being a member of a church which pays its bills in full every month. He has also conducted League evangelistic services with great success. A few years ago he was nominated by the Prohibition party of Nebraska as a candidate for governor of the State.

PINER, REV. W. K., is pastor of the State Street M. E. Church South, Bowling Green, Ky. Was born in Texas in 1862, and entered the ministry in 1882. During his pastorate at Bowling Green a new church costing $40,000 has been built. He has held revival services in a number of States and Conferences. Mr. Piner is corresponding editor of the *Central Methodist*, Kettlesburg, Ky.

PIPER, HON. C. E., is General Treasurer of the Epworth League in the Methodist Episcopal Church. He was born June 12th, 1858, in Chicago, Ill. Educated at Northwestern University and at Union Law College, Chicago, Mr. Piper has been prominent in League work since its organization. He is a member of the Board of Control and a Director of Epworth League Children's Home. Is a member of the law firm of Andrews & Piper.

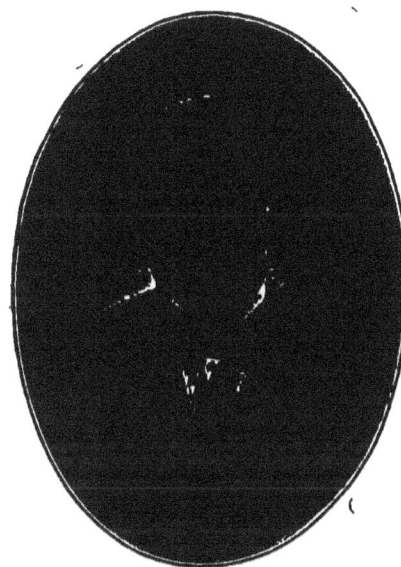

HON. C. E. PIPER.

PLANTZ, MRS. MYRA GOODWIN, is wife of Dr. Samuel Plantz, President of Lawrence University, Appleton, Wis. Mrs. Plantz has made a specialty of children's work, on which subject she spoke at the Cleveland Convention, and this year at the Wisconsin State Convention. She has also been much interested in the Mercy and Help Department and the Social work of the League. She gives part of the time to literary work, her most frequent contributions appearing in the *Epworth Herald*, though she is a contributor to a number of publications. She has published in book form two stories for young people, "Corner Work" and "A Great Appointment." In the League of the Appleton Church Mrs. Plantz is an interested worker.

PENN, MR. IRVINE G., is Assistant Secretary of the Epworth League of the Methodist Episcopal Church. He was appointed at the last meeting of the Board of Control to work especially among the colored chapters. Rev. Dr. Schell says of him: "Mr. Penn, the new Assistant Secretary chosen with special reference for our Southern work, is justifying every hour the wisdom of having such an officer, and his special fitness for the work."

PERRIN, REV. WILLIARD T., is President of the First General District of the Epworth League, which includes most of New England, and is pastor of the First Methodist Episcopal Church, Boston, Mass. He was born in 1850. In 1870 graduated from Harvard College, and subsequently took the degree of S.T.B. in Boston University School of Theology. His appointments have been Wilbraham, Springfield, Charleston, Worcester, Lowell and Boston, where he is now serving for the fifth year. In 1885 he was made a Trustee of Boston University. Mr. Perrin is brother-in-law of Mr. W. E. H. Massey, of Toronto.

REV. JOHN POTTS, D.D.

POTTS, REV. JOHN, D.D., was born in Ireland, in 1838. He came to this country while still a lad. His education, when a boy, was that of the schools of his native land, and soon after coming to Canada he entered Victoria College to prepare for the work of the ministry. He has been the pastor of the leading churches in Toronto, Hamilton and Montreal, and these churches have, when possible, secured his services for a second term. He was pastor of the Metropolitan Church, Toronto, for six years. He has been President of Conference, and is now the General Secretary of Education for the Methodist Church of Canada. He is also Chairman of the International Sunday School Lesson Committee.

PUTNAM, MISS GRACE, is a teacher in the High School, Chattanooga, Tenn. She is a member of the First M. E. Church in Chattanooga, and has been specially interested in the Mercy and Help Department of the Epworth League and in mission Sunday School work.

RACE, REV. JOHN H., A.M., is pastor of the Centenary M. E. Church, Binghamton, N.Y., now beginning his fourth year. He was born in the State of Pennsylvania in 1862, graduating from Princeton College. From 1890 to 1894 he occupied a position as teacher in the Wyoming Seminary. He is at present president of the Wyoming Conference Epworth League.

RADER, REV. L. S., D.D., was born in Ohio, and entered the East Ohio Conference in 1882, where he served the following charges : Warrensville, Madison, Twinsburg, New Athens, and Woodland Avenue, Cleveland. He was then transferred to the St. John's River Conference, and was made presiding elder of Entis District. After three and a half years on this district he was appointed pastor of Trinity Church, Jacksonville, Fla.; from thence he was transferred to be pastor at Greenville, Pa. He was a member of the last General Conference.

RAMSAY, REV. E. B., is pastor of the Hernando Street M. E. Church South, Memphis, Tenn.; was born in Bedford, Tenn., and educated in Jacinto College, North Mississippi. Has been stationed at Jackson, Tenn., Union City, Tenn., and Paducah, Ky. Has given special attention to temperance and revival work.

RAMSEY, MR. JOE M., is field-secretary and organizer of Epworth Leagues in the Tennessee Conference of the M. E. Church South. He is four feet, eleven inches in height, weighs one hundred pounds, has the appearance of a boy about fifteen years old, and is totally blind. He manages, however, to do an immense amount of Epworth League work. He has organized one hundred Leagues, with a membership of about four thousand. He has travelled ten thousand miles in the interest of the League, about half of that through the country. Last year he secured five hundred subscriptions to the *Epworth Era*. He lives at Viola, Tenn.

RANTON, REV. A. H., is an evangelist. He was born in St. John, N.B., in 1863, and was educated in the Ontario public and collegiate schools. He entered the ministry in Canada, July, 1884. He has served in several pastorates, and has been very successful in revival work. Mr. Ranton now resides at Kalamazoo, Mich.; but, inasmuch as he was born in Canada, entered the ministry in Canada, and his work for the past two years having been mostly in this country, he appears on the programme as one of the Canadian speakers.

RAWLINGS, REV. E. H., A.M., is pastor of the Clay Street M. E. Church South, Virginia, and President of the State Epworth League Conference. He was born in the State of Virginia in 1865, and graduated from Randolph Macon College. He is the author of a little book entitled "The Pastor and the League," recently issued by the Publishing House of the M. E. Church South.

REDDITT, REV. J. J., is pastor of St. Paul's Methodist Church, Brampton. Was born in Toronto in 1853, and entered the ministry in 1877. He has been District Secretary, Financial Secretary, and Secretary of Conference. Has given special attention to Sunday School work and the Department of Spiritual Work in the League.

RICE, MR. BRUCE L., is city attorney for the city of Clarksville, Tenn., and is also in the regular practice of law. He is Assistant Sunday School Superintendent, and Chairman of the Literary Department of the League in the Madison Street M. E. Church South. He is the son of a Methodist preacher, the brother of a Methodist preacher, and the nephew of six Methodist preachers. He was born in 1870. His father, the Rev. J. G. Rice, is a member of the Tennessee Conference.

RICE, REV. J. A., D.D., was born in South Carolina, September 25, 1862. Graduated from South Carolina College in 1885. Taught in this college until 1889, when he entered the ministry of the Methodist Episcopal Church South. Has been stationed at Darlington and Columbia. From the latter place he was called to the presidency of the Columbia Female College, which position he now holds. The honorary degree of D.D. was conferred upon him by his *Alma Mater* in 1894.

RICHARDS, REV. E. H., is Superintendent of Missions in East Africa for the Methodist Episcopal Church. Has done considerable work in the way of primary explorations in East Africa, has founded several stations, and translated the entire New Testament into the Tonga dialect. While in America on two visits he has delivered more than 1,000 lectures on "Home Life in Eastern Africa," and "Explorations in the Dark Continent."

RIDDELL, REV. J. H., B.A., B.D., is lecturer in Classics, Biblical Theology and New Testament Exegesis, in Wesley College, Winnipeg, Man. In 1885 he matriculated with honors in English in Toronto University, but took his course in Victoria University, graduating in Arts in 1890, winning several prizes. He entered the ministry in the Manitoba and North-West Conference. In 1892 the Conference appointed him to the double work of pastor of Young Church, a newly organized society in the city, and lecturer in Classics in Wesley College, which dual work he prosecuted with eminent success until last July, when he was appointed to his present position. Prof. Riddell is President of the Manitoba Conference Epworth League.

RIKER, REV. A. B., is pastor of the State Street M. E. Church, Charleston, W.Va. He was born in Columbus, Ohio, October 19th, 1852, and graduated from the Ohio Wesleyan University, receiving the degree of D.D. from this university in 1888. He has been stationed in Columbus and Athens, O., Chattanooga, Tenn., Wheeling, W.Va.

ROBINSON, MISS JULIA A., was born in Dubuque, Iowa, and educated in the Public schools there, graduating from the High School. At present she occupies the position of Office Secretary in the Central office of the Epworth League at Chicago. She is specially interested in Junior work, and writes the Junior notes for the *Epworth Herald*.

ROSE, REV. S. P., D.D., is pastor of St. James Methodist Church, Montreal, Canada, one of the largest and finest church edifices in Methodism. He is the son of the late Rev. Dr. Rose, for many years Book Steward of the Canadian Methodist Church, and was born in 1853, in the County of Middlesex. In 1872, he received the degree of D.D. from the Wesleyan Theological College in Montreal, in which institution he has been a lecturer. Dr. Rose has always taken an active interest in young people's work. He has been president of local and provincial unions of the Christian Endeavor Society, and is now President of the Montreal Conference Epworth League.

ROYAL, REV. STANLEY OLIN, of Troy, O., was born in Libertyville, Ill., in the year 1851. His preparation for the ministry was received at Drew Theological Seminary, Madison, N.J., taking his degree of B.D. in 1877. He joined the Cincinnati Conference in 1877, and has been in the pastoral work ever since. For ten years he has been Secretary of this Conference. His interest in and success with young people led to his appointment in 1892 as a member of the General Board of Control of the Epworth League, and his re-appointment in 1896.

RYCKMAN, REV. E. B., D.D., is pastor of the Queen Street Methodist Church, Kingston, Ont. He has been stationed in some of the most important pulpits in Canadian Methodism, among which may be mentioned London, Paris, Ottawa and Montreal. Dr. Ryckman has also been the President of the London and Montreal conferences.

SALTON, REV. GEORGE F., Ph.B., is pastor of the First Methodist Church, St. Thomas, Ont. He was born in England in 1858, educated in the Wesleyan Academy, West Hartlepool, Eng. Came to Canada in 1881. Intended to follow his profession as Art Teacher, but entered the ministry in 1882. Has been stationed at Chesley, Clinton, Goderich, Waterloo, Brussels, Strathroy and St. Thomas. Mr. Salton is now giving special attention to Junior League work, and spends every Saturday afternoon with the Juniors personally. His Junior League numbers 225. He is to appear on the Chautauqua New York platform this summer.

SAUNDERS, REV. J. B., M.D., D.D., is pastor of the Dominion Methodist Church, Ottawa. He was born in England fifty years ago and received his early education in the Mother-land. He came to Canada and entered the Methodist ministry in 1868. He has been pastor of three churches in Montreal, Governor of Stanstead College, and Professor in Bishop's College, Montreal. He has also been stationed in Pembroke, Brockville and Ottawa. In addition to his medical degree, Victoria University conferred upon him the degree of D.D. at the last meeting of its Senate.

SCHELL, REV. EDWIN A., D D., General Secretary of the Epworth League of the Methodist Episcopal Church. He is a graduate of Northwestern University. Previous to his present position he was the successful pastor of a large church in Yonkers, N.Y. Since his appointment as General Secretary he has shown great energy in developing the various departments of the Epworth League. The success of the Epworth League Reading Course is largely due to his efforts.

REV. DR. SCHELL.

SCHOYER, MR. A. M., is a layman connected with the Linden Avenue M. E. Church, Allegheny City, Pa., and President of the Fourth General Conference District Epworth League, which is composed of seven of the largest conferences. He is Superintendent of Telegraph of the Pennsylvania lines west of Pittsburg, Vandalia Line, and the Grand Rapids and Indiana Railway Company, and has been connected with the railway business all his life.

SCOTT, REV. C. T., was born in the village of Stouffville, Ont., in 1860, started in life for himself at thirteen years of age in a grocery store, from which he graduated into the ministry in 1881. Received his education in Wesleyan College, Montreal, and Victoria University, Cobourg. Has been stationed at West Lorne, Dutton and St. Thomas.

SCOTT, MISS E. J., is superintendent of the Deaconess work in the city of Toronto. She was born in Baltimore, Md. Was brought up in the Episcopal Church, but after her conversion joined the Methodist Church. For the past seven years she has been a Deaconess, doing district visiting and special work among children.

SELLERY, REV. S., B.D., is pastor of Dublin Street Methodist Church, Guelph, was born at Carleton Place, 1849, and educated at Victoria College, Cobourg. Has been Chairman of District, President of the Hamilton Conference Epworth League, Secretary of Hamilton Conference and representative on the Sunday School and Epworth League Board.

SHOAFF, REV. J. W., D.D., began to preach at the early age of nineteen years, and has filled important charges in Virginia, Baltimore and Alabama conferences. During his pastorate at St. Paul's Church, Baltimore, he found it necessary to seek a more equable climate, and was transferred to the Alabama Conference and stationed at St. Francis Street Church in the city of Mobile, which is one of the most important charges in the State. He is now pastor of the First M. E. Church South in Selma. The degree of D.D. was conferred upon him by the Southern University located at Greensboro', Ala., some two years ago.

SLUTZ, REV. W. B., D.D., is pastor of the First M. E. Church, Wichita, Kan. He was born in 1856 and entered the ministry in 1881. He holds the degree of B.A. from Mount Union College, Alliance, O., and D.D. from Baker University, Baldwin, Kan. He is the originator of the May and Autumn festival idea, which consists of a course of lectures and attractive music under the direction of the Literary Department.

SMILEY, MRS. ANNIE E., Milford, Mass., was born in the State of Massachusetts, and graduated from Drew Ladies' Seminary, Carmel, N.Y. She is a member of the Milford M. E. Church, of which her husband, Rev. G. M. Smiley, is pastor. Mrs. Smiley has given special attention to the Junior and Primary work of the Church. She is well known as the author of "Fifty Social Evenings," a valuable book for the use of fourth vice-presidents of the Epworth Leagues, and is at present at work on another book, entitled "Junior Methods and Programmes."

SMITH, REV. A. COKE, D.D., is pastor of the M. E. Church South, Lynchburg, Va. Was born in South Carolina, 1849, and graduated from Wofford College, Spartanburg, S.C. Has been pastor on stations in the South Carolina Conference, presiding elder, professor in Wofford College, and also professor in Vanderbilt University. In 1890, at the General Conference held in St. Louis, Mo., Dr. Smith was elected one of the missionary secretaries of his Church, which position he resigned to accept a professorship in Vanderbilt University. In 1892 he left college work to enter the pastorate again, and was sent to Granby Street, Norfolk, Pa., which station he filled for four years, the limit of the pastoral term in the M. E. Church.

SMITH, REV. J. V., D.D., is pastor of the Centenary Methodist Church, Hamilton, Canada. He was born in Cumberland, Eng., and entered the ministry in 1870. Has been stationed in Windsor, London, Galt, Toronto and Hamilton. Previous to his present appointment he was pastor of the Metropolitan Church, Toronto. Dr. Smith has published a valuable little booklet on "The Church and the Boys."

SNYDER, HENRY N., M.A., is a member of the Central M. E. Church South, Spartanburg, S.C. He was born in Macon, Ga., January

14th, 1865, and educated at Vanderbilt University. He is now Professor of English Language and Literature in Wofford College, Spartanburg.

SOLOMON, MRS. W. G., is Third Vice-President of the Georgia State League, and Assistant Superintendent of the Sunday School in the Mulberry Street M. E. Church South, Macon, Ga. She was born in Macon and educated at the Wesleyan Female College there.

SPARLING, REV. W., B.D., is pastor of the Methodist Church in he city of Quebec, Canada. He was born in Renfrew County, Canada, and educated in McGill University and Wesleyan Theological College, Montreal. Has been stationed at Kingston, St. Lambert, Westmount, Easton's Corners, Montreal Conference, and has supplied the pulpit of St. James Church, Montreal, on two occasions. He has received invitations to the Dominion Church, Ottawa, and to Parkdale Methodist Church, Toronto.

STEEL, REV. S. A., D.D., General Secretary of the Epworth League of the Methodist Episcopal Church South, and editor of the *Epworth Era*. Previous to his appointment he filled pastorates in Richmond, Nashville, Memphis and Kansas City. He has travelled extensively through the United States and Canada in the interest of the League. In addition to his writing in the *Era* he has published two racy books of travel, "On the Wing" and "On the Rail," in which he gives considerable interesting information about the places which he has visited and the people he has met.

REV. DR. STEEL.

STEPHENSON, MR. F. C., is a medical student of Trinity College, Toronto, preparing for work in the mission field. He is the originator of the "Students' Missionary Campaign" in the Methodist Church, Canada, and editor of *The Campaigner*, a monthly paper devoted to missionary work.

SPENCE, MR. F. S., is an alderman of the city of Toronto, and a member of the Parliament Street Church. For many years he has given special attention to temperance work, and there is probably no one in Canada better posted on this subject. At present he is Secretary of the Dominion Alliance.

STARR, MR. J. R. L., LL.B., is one of Toronto's successful lawyers. He is at present Superintendent of the Sunday School of Bathurst Street Methodist Church. Has been President of the Toronto City Union of Methodist Young People's Societies, and also President of the Toronto Conference Epworth League. He is at present a Public School Trustee for the city, and is President of the Toronto Football Association.

SUTHERLAND, REV. ALEX., D.D., is General Secretary of Missions for the Methodist Church in Canada. He was born near Guelph, Ont., in 1833. When he was nine years of age his father died, and at thirteen he was forced to leave home and earn his own living. In 1859 he was received into full connection with the Conference and ordained. During his pastorate he was stationed at Niagara, Thorold, Drummond, Hamilton, Toronto and Montreal. At the first General Conference of the Methodist Church of Canada, in 1874, Dr. Sutherland was elected General Secretary and Clerical Treasurer of the Missionary Society, as successor to the Rev. Lachlan Taylor, D.D. During Dr. Sutherland's term of office the Missionary income of the Church has increased from $118,000 to nearly $250,000. He has been president of the Toronto Conference twice, representative to the Ecumenical Conference, London, England, and fraternal delegate to the British Wesleyan Conference and to the General Conference of the M. E. Church South. He has been selected by the Theological Faculty of the Vanderbilt University and the Board of Bishops of the M. E. Church South to deliver a course of lectures on the "Cole Foundation."

REV. ALEX. SUTHERLAND, D.D.

STOUT, REV. J. FRANK, D.D., was born in New York in 1850. He was educated at the Northwestern University, Evanston, Ill., from which he has since received the degrees of A.M. and D.D. He has served important stations in the Illinois and Minnesota conferences, and is at present pastor of the First M. E. Church, St. Paul, Minn. He has been President of the Minnesota State Epworth League, and also editor of the Epworth League department in the *Methodist Herald*.

STUART, REV. J. M., is pastor of the First Methodist Episcopal Church, Carthage, Mo. He was born at Washington, Ohio, educated at Baker University, and entered the ministry in 1881. He was a member of the last General Conference, has been presiding elder, and is now President of the Inter-State Chautauqua Assembly, located at Carthage, Mo.

SWADENER, REV. MADISON, is Superintendent of the Cincinnati Church Extension Society ; was Y.M.C.A. General Secretary before entering the ministry. He was born in 1852, entered the ministry in 1872, and spent eleven years in the regular pastorate. He has given special attention to revival work in connection with the Epworth League, and has made careful study of city life in the United States. The society of which he is the superintendent is a part of the great city evangelistic movement of the Methodist Episcopal Church.

SWARTHOUT, ELVIN, LL.B., is Secretary of the Epworth League Assembly at Ludington, Michigan, and is a member of the Division Street M. E. Church, Grand Rapids, Mich. Was born in Ovid, Mich., October 5th, 1864, graduating from Albion College in 1885 with the degree of Ph.D. Admitted to the Bar of the Supreme Court, Michigan, 1886, and graduated from the University of Michigan in 1887. Has been practising law in Grand Rapids ever since. Was State President of the Epworth League from 1893 to 1894, and a lay delegate to the last General Conference held at Cleveland.

SWENERTON, MR. B. F., is Secretary of the Nova Scotia Conference Epworth League, and Assistant Superintendent of the Grafton Street Methodist Sunday School, Halifax, N.S. He has been a Sunday School teacher for a number of years, also local preacher and Recording Steward. At present he is in the brokerage and commission business at Halifax, N.S.

SWITZER, REV. GEORGE W., is pastor of the West LaFayette M. E. Church, Indiana, and President of the LaFayette District Epworth League. Was born in Indiana, 1854, graduated from University at Grand Castle, Ind., 1881. Entered the ministry in 1880. Was a delegate to the International Conference Y.M.C.A., held in London, Eng., in 1881.

THOBURN, REV. J. M., Jun., is a nephew of Bishop Thoburn, and is stationed at Central M. E. Church, Detroit, Mich. He was born at St. Clairsville, Ohio, in 1856, and was educated at Alleghany College,

Meadville, Pa. During his ministry he has been stationed ta the following charges: English Church, Calcutta, India; Trinity Church, Oil City, Pa., and First Church, Duluth, Minn.

THIRKIELD, REV. W. P., D.D., is President of Gammon Theological Seminary, Atlanta, Ga, which Bishop Haygood has 'pronounced to be the most important and successful undertaking in the education of ministers, especially for the negro race in America or in the world. Mr. Thirkield began this work in 1883, with two students and an endowment of $20,000. The institution now has an attendance of over ninety students and an endowment of more than half a million dollars, with library and other buildings and equipments worth one hundred thousand dollars. Mr. Thirkield was born in Franklin, Ohio, September 25th, 1854. He is a graduate of the Ohio University, and the Boston University School of Theology. He has done much pulpit and platform work throughout the South, and has been an earnest worker in temperance, educational, Sunday School and League work.

REV. DR. THIRKIELD.

THORNTON, DR. A. W., is a dentist in Chatham, Ont. Was born in the town of Perth, 1858, taught school for thirteen years, after which he studied dentistry and obtained a license from the Royal College of Dental Surgery and his degree from Toronto University. Dr. Thornton is President of the London Conference Epworth League, a local preacher in the Methodist Church, and a teacher of the Park Street Bible Class, Chatham, having a membership of about three hundred, probably the largest in the Province.

THORPE, REV. ERVIN LLEWELLYN, D.D., D.C.L., was born in Malden, Ill., September 2nd, 1857. Graduated A.B. from Baker University, LL.B. from Iowa State University, D.T.B. and D.C.L. from Yale University. Dr. Thorpe was Vice-President of Upper Iowa University for two years, practised law in Iowa for two years, joined Upper Iowa Conference in 1879, and transferred to New York East Conference in 1885. He was pastor for five years of First Methodist Episcopal Church, Hartford, Conn., and at present pastor of Washington Park Methodist Episcopal Church, Bridgeport, Conn.

TIGERT, REV. J. J., D.D., is Book Editor of the M. E. Church South Publishing House, Nashville, Tenn., and is also editor of the *Methodist Review*. He was born in Louisville, Ky., in 1856, and educated at Vanderbilt University. He has been pastor for eight years, professor in Vanderbilt University nine years, and editor three years. He is the author of a "Constitutional History of American Episcopal Methodism."

TUNNELL, MR. F. W., is a manufacturer in Philadelphia, Pa. Has been superintendent of the First M. E. Church Sunday School, Germantown, Philadelphia, for over twelve years, also trustee of the church and chairman of all its financial work, including the new building now in course of erection, which will be one of the finest churches in Philadelphia.

TURK, REV. G. R., is pastor of Grace Church, Winnipeg, Manitoba, where he has been stationed for five years. He has been transferred to Toronto Conference, and at the time of the Convention it is expected that he will be pastor of Carlton Street Church. He has been stationed at Goderich, Guelph and Owen Sound.

VAN CLEVE, REV. JOSEPH W., was born in Illinois in 1859, educated at McKendree College at Lebanon, and entered the ministry in 1880. He was appointed pastor of the Church at Mount Vernon, Ill., and is a member of the General Board of Control of the Epworth League of the M. E. Church. He is secretary of the Southern Illinois Conference, and was a member of the last General Conference.

WAILES, REV. J. A., was born in Missouri in 1863, entered the ministry in 1884 in the Missouri Conference of the M. E. Church South ; has preached in Warrentown, Wright City, Monticello, Clarence, Albany, Savannah ; is now presiding elder of the St. Charles District, residing at Wentzville, Mo. He is vice-president of the Missouri Conference Epworth League Board, and was president of the Board which drafted the Missouri Conference League constitution.

WATCH, REV. C. W., is pastor of the Methodist Church, Brighton ; was born in England in 1850, and received a commercial English education. At present he is secretary of the Bay of Quinte Conference Epworth League, financial secretary of the Brighton District, a member of the General Epworth League Board, and superintendent of Canadian child-saving work. Mr. Watch has given special attention to the work of child-saving.

WALDEN, REV. JOHN M., D.D., is Bishop of the Methodist Episcopal Church. He was born in Lebanon, O., on February 11th, 1831, and spent his early life on a farm; afterward, while engaged as a clerk, he devoted his leisure time to reading, and later he entered Farmer's College, graduating in the year 1852. He was immediately appointed to a tutorship, and two years later became interested in a journalistic enterprise. He served as a member of the Legislature, and was elected State Superintendent of Public Instruction. Converted in 1850, he was soon after licensed as a local preacher, and in 1858 was admitted into the Cincinnati Conference. He soon rose to command prominent appointments. He became Corresponding Secretary of the Western Freedman's Aid Society, and was so engaged until the formation of the Freedman's Aid Society, of which he was one of the foremost movers and its first corresponding secretary. While presiding elder of the East Cincinnati District, in 1868, he was elected agent of the Western Book Concern, and was re-elected in 1872, 1876 and 1880. In 1884 he was elected to the highest office in the gift of the Church. Bishop Walden has been a prolific writer on temperance and education, and lectured extensively on these subjects. He was also a prominent member of the Ecumenical Conference in London in 1881.

BISHOP WALDEN.

WERLEIN, REV. J. H., D.D., is pastor of the LaFayette Park M. E. Church South, St. Louis, Mo.; was born in the State of Mississippi in 1851; educated at Drew Theological Seminary, and entered the ministry of the St. Louis Conference in 1875. He has been pastor in New Orleans, Houston, Texas, and in 1894 was presiding elder of the St. Louis District. He is now serving his second term in the pastorate of LaFayette church. In 1889 he received the degree of D.D. Dr. Werlein was a delegate to the Ecumenical Conference held in City Road Chapel, London, Eng., in 1881.

WESTHAFFER, REV. S. T., is pastor of the First Methodist Episcopal Church, Chattanooga; was born in Tracy, Ohio, 1865; graduated from the Ohio Wesleyan University, Delaware, in 1891, and also from Boston University School of Theology, 1893. Entered the Maine Conference in 1893, and was stationed at Wesley Church, Baltimore, the second largest church in the Conference.

WHITTLE, W. O., is a member of the First M. E. Church, Knoxville, N.C., and holds a position with the Knoxville Banking Company. He was formerly editor of the *Epworthian*, a local Epworth League paper, and is now president of the Epworth League, assistant superintendent of the Sunday School, and a member of the Board of Trustees.

WILSON, REV. W. F., is pastor of Wesley Church, Hamilton, Ont. He was born in Toronto about forty years ago, entered the ministry in 1879. Has been stationed at Woodgreen, McCaul and Trinity churches, Toronto. Mr. Wilson was one of the speakers at the Washington Christian Endeavor Convention.

WOODCOCK, HON. WILLIAM L., is an official member of the First M. E. Church, Altoona, Pa., and a member of the General Board of Control of the Epworth League. He is also President of the local League at Altoona, and for three years was honored with the presidency of the Fourth General Conference District, which embraced several states. He has given special attention to Sunday School work. Seven years ago he erected Belenore Hall and started a mission Sunday School with fifteen scholars, which now numbers four hundred. He is superintendent of this school. Mr. Woodcock is a lawyer by profession.

PATTEN, MR J. A., is not on the Programme, but he has had much to do with its preparation, having acted as Secretary of the Methodist Episcopal section of the Programme Committee. He will be remembered by those who were at Chattanooga in 1895, as the very efficient General Secretary of the local committee. He probably did more than any other one man toward making that great gathering a success. Mr. Patten is a member of the First Methodist Episcopal Church of Chattanooga. He joined the Epworth League in 1889 and has been President of his chapter, City Union and District League, is now President of the Holston Conference League, and a member of the General Board of Control. Mr. Patten was for a long time editor of the League Department of the *Methodist Advocate-Journal* and is a director of the company which publishes that paper. He is a trustee of U. S. Grant University.

MR. J. A. PATTEN.

The Music.

Special attention will be given to congregational singing during the Convention, and with a view to this a number of selections have been made from well-known standard hymns, which are familiar everywhere. Variety will be provided for by the introduction of several pieces from the new book, "Songs for Young People," plates of which have been kindly supplied by Messrs. Curts & Jennings, Publishers, Cincinnati, O.

The following city organists have kindly consented to officiate: Mrs. Powell, Mrs. A. W. Austin and Miss Brown, and Messrs. E. R. Doward, A. Hewitt, T. Arthur Miller, A. Jordan, W. A. Cork, J. N. Shannon, Harry West and Mrs. Jury.

Two cornetists, highly recommended, are coming from the United States, Rev. M. A. Harlan, of Logansport, Ind., and Miss Lottie Michael, of Elkhart, Ind.; these with several Toronto cornetists will assist the leaders in congregational singing.

The choirs and singers from the Toronto Epworth Leagues are being grouped in four large choruses, each under the leadership of an experienced and able conductor, namely :

IN THE METROPOLITAN CHURCH.

MR. F. H. TORRINGTON, for about twenty-five years the organist and choir-master of the Metropolitan Church. Mr. Torrington was formerly organist and choir-director of King's Chapel, Boston ; conductor in association with Carl Zerrahn and Mr. Gilmore, of the mass rehearsals of the great chorus of the last Boston Jubilee ; Professor of Piano, New England Conservatory of Music, Boston ; Solo Organist of Boston Music Hall and Plymouth Church, Brooklyn (Henry Ward Beecher's). Mr. Torrington came to Toronto in 1873, where he has been, without doubt, the father of oratorio and orchestral music. He organized the Toronto Philharmonic Society, and produced before the public the standard oratorios, cantatas and miscellaneous works of the great composers, many of them for the first time in Canada ; organized and conducted the Toronto Musical Festival of 1886, an unprecedented musical and financial success, and the festival given at the opening of the Massey Music Hall ; founded the Toronto College of Music (affiliated with the University of Toronto), Toronto Orchestra and the Toronto Orchestral School.

IN MASSEY HALL.

MR. E. O. EXCELL is well known as a popular leader of music in great evangelistic services. Toronto people will remember him in connection with the meetings held by Rev. Sam. P. Jones many years ago. Mr. Excell has published a number of music books, among which may be mentioned "Excell's Anthems," "Triumphant Songs," and last of all, "Songs for Young People," which has just been issued by the Western Methodist Book Concern, Cincinnati and Chicago. This book will be used at the Massey Hall meetings, and may be purchased by all desiring to take a copy home with them. Mr. Excell will sing solos at the services, and will also render several duets with Prof. C. H. Gabriel, of Chicago.

IN COOKE'S CHURCH.

MR. A. T. CRINGAN, the choir-master of the Church and, for many years past, the chief instructor of singing in the Public Schools of Toronto, and the most prominent Canadian exponent of the Tonic Sol-Fa System.

IN THE PAVILION.

MR. J. M. SHERLOCK, the Principal of the vocal department of the Metropolitan School of Music, Toronto; choir-master of Trinity Methodist Church, and the solo tenor of Kingston Philharmonic Society. Mr. Sherlock is organizing an orchestra to play in the Pavilion during the Convention.

The Pianos used at Convention meetings will be supplied by Messrs. Mason & Risch, Music Dealers, King Street West.

Master CLAUDE SANER, of Iowa, and Master BERNEY RAUTENBERG, two gifted boy vocalists and Junior Leaguers, will render solos.

ORGAN AND CHOIR, METROPOLITAN CHURCH.

23. Holy, Holy, Holy! Lord God Almighty! (NICÆA.—11, 12, 12, 10.)

3 Holy, holy, holy! though the darkness hide thee,
Though the eye of sinful man thy glory may not see,
Only thou art holy; there is none beside thee
Perfect in power, in love, and purity!

4 Holy, holy, holy, Lord God Almighty!
All thy works shall praise thy name, in earth and sky and sea:
Holy, holy, holy, merciful and mighty,
God in three persons, blessed Trinity!

—*Bishop Heber.*

He Leadeth Me. (4-8s.)

1. He leadeth me! oh, blessed thought, Oh, words with heav'nly comfort fraught; What e'er I do, where'er I be, Still 'tis God's hand that leadeth me.

2. Sometimes 'mid scenes of deepest gloom, Sometimes where Eden's bowers bloom, By waters still, o'er troubled sea,—Still 'tis his hand that leadeth me.

CHORUS — He leadeth me, he leadeth me, By his own hand he leadeth me; His faithful follower I would be, For by his hand he leadeth me.

3 Lord, I would clasp thy hand in mine,
Nor ever murmur nor repine—
Content, whatever lot I see,
Since 'tis my God that leadeth me.

4 And when my task on earth is done,
When, by thy grace, the victory's won,
E'en death's cold wave I will not flee,
Since God through Jordan leadeth me.
—*J. H. Gilmore.*

50. Oh, Safe to the Rock that is Higher than I. (11s.)

Words by REV. W. O. CUSHING. IRA D. SANKEY.

1. Oh, safe to the Rock that is high-er than I, My soul in its con-flicts and sor-rows would fly; So sin-ful, so wea-ry, thine, thine would I be; Thou blest "Rock of A-ges," I'm hid-ing in thee.
2. In the calm of the noon-tide, in sor-row's lone hour, In times when temp-ta-tion casts o'er me its power; In the tem-pests of life, on its wide, heav-ing sea, Thou blest "Rock of A-ges," I'm hid-ing in thee.
3. How oft in the con-flict, when pressed by the foe, I have fled to my Ref-uge and breathed out my woe; How of-ten when tri-als, like sea bil-lows roll, Have I hid-den in thee, O thou Rock of my soul.

CHORUS.

Hid-ing in thee, Hid-ing in thee, Thou blest "Rock of Ages," I'm hid-ing in thee

51. How Firm a Foundation. (ADESTE FIDELES.—11s.)

M. PORTOGALLO.

1. How firm a foun-da-tion, ye saints of the Lord, Is laid for your faith in his ex-cel-lent word! What more can he say, than to you he hath said,.. To you, who for ref-uge to Je-sus have fled; To you, who for ref-uge to Je-sus have fled?

2. "Fear not, I am with thee; Oh, be not dismayed! For I am thy God, I will still give thee aid; I'll strengthen thee, help thee, and cause thee to stand, Up-held by my gra-cious, om-nip-o-tent hand; Up-held by my gra-cious, om-nip-o-tent hand.

3. "When through the deep waters I call thee to go,
The rivers of sorrow shall not overflow;
For I will be with thee thy trials to bless,
And sanctify to thee thy deepest distress.

4. "When through fiery trials thy pathway shall lie,
My grace, all-sufficient, shall be thy supply;
The flame shall not hurt thee; I only design
Thy dross to consume, and thy gold to refine."

—G. Keith.

130 Come, Ye that Love the Lord. (NEARER HOME.—S.M.D.)

Words by ISAAC WATTS.   ISAAC WOODBURY.
Moderate

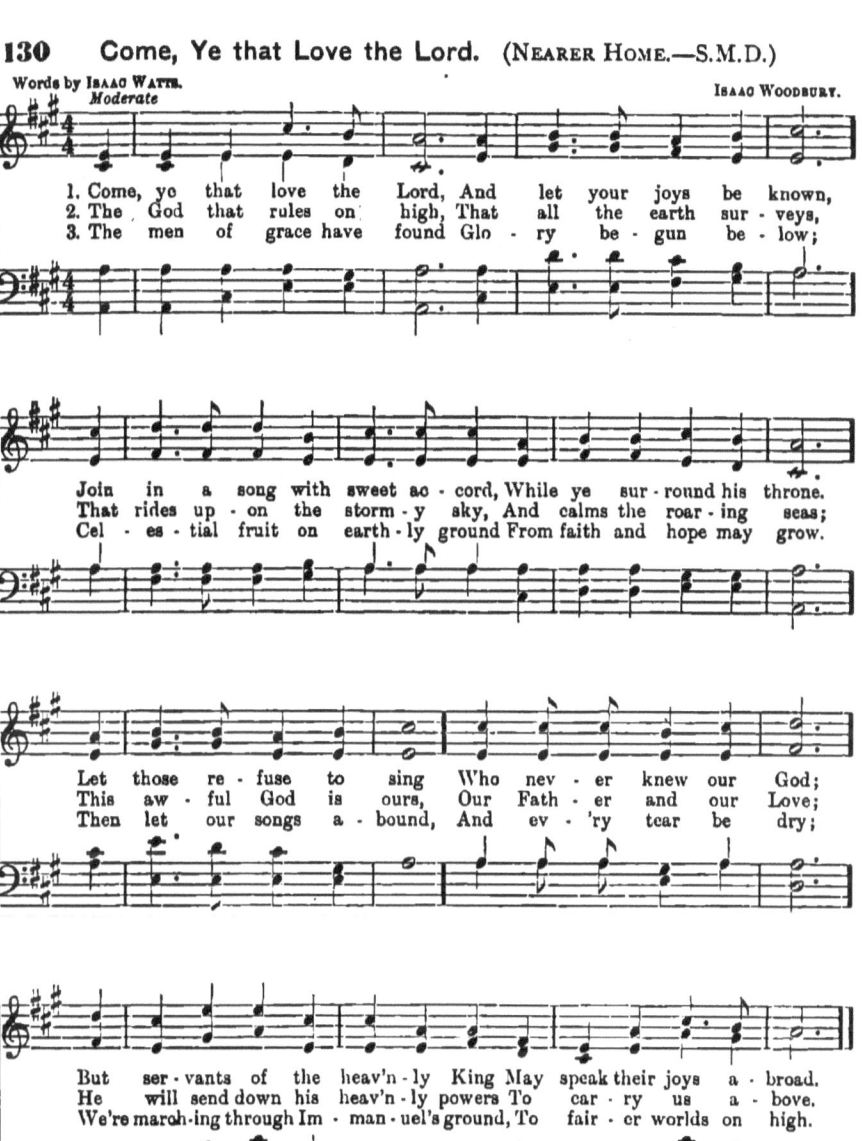

1. Come, ye that love the Lord, And let your joys be known,
2. The God that rules on high, That all the earth sur-veys,
3. The men of grace have found Glo-ry be-gun be-low;

Join in a song with sweet ac-cord, While ye sur-round his throne.
That rides up-on the storm-y sky, And calms the roar-ing seas;
Cel-es-tial fruit on earth-ly ground From faith and hope may grow.

Let those re-fuse to sing Who nev-er knew our God;
This aw-ful God is ours, Our Fath-er and our Love;
Then let our songs a-bound, And ev-'ry tear be dry;

But ser-vants of the heav'n-ly King May speak their joys a-broad.
He will send down his heav'n-ly powers To car-ry us a-bove.
We're march-ing through Im-man-uel's ground, To fair-er worlds on high.

131. Blest be the Tie that Binds. (DENNIS.—S.M.)

HANS GEORGE NAEGELI

1. Blest be the tie that binds Our hearts in Christian love;
   The fellowship of kindred minds Is like to that above.
2. Before our Father's throne, We pour our ardent prayers;
   Our fears, our hopes, our aims are one, Our comforts and our cares.

3 We share our mutual woes,
  Our mutual burdens bear;
  And often for each other flows
  The sympathizing tear.

4 From sorrow, toil, and pain,
  And sin we shall be free;
  And perfect love and friendship reign
  Through all eternity.
  —*J. Fawcett.*

108. A Charge to Keep I Have. (S.M.—TUNE NO. 131.)

1 A charge to keep I have,
  A God to glorify,
  A never-dying soul to save,
  And fit it for the sky.

2 To serve the present age,
  My calling to fulfil;
  Oh, may it all my pow'rs engage
  To do my Master's will!

3 Arm me with jealous care,
  As in thy sight to live;
  And oh, thy servant, Lord, prepare,
  A strict account to give!

4 Help me to watch and pray,
  And on thyself rely;
  Assured, if I my trust betray,
  I shall for ever die.
  —*C. Wesley.*

320. Lord, if at Thy Command. (S.M.—TUNE. NO. 131.)

1 Lord, if at thy command
  The word of life we sow,
  Watered by thy almighty hand,
  The seed shall surely grow.

2 The virtue of thy grace
  A large increase shall give,
  And multiply the faithful race
  Who to thy glory live.

3 Now then the ceaseless shower
  Of gospel blessings send,
  And let the soul-converting power
  Thy ministers attend.

4 On multitudes confer
  The heart-renewing love,
  And by the joy of grace prepare
  For fuller joys above.
  —*C. Wesley.*

157 Happy the Man who Finds the Grace. (HURSLEY.—L.M.)

HUGUENOT MELODY.

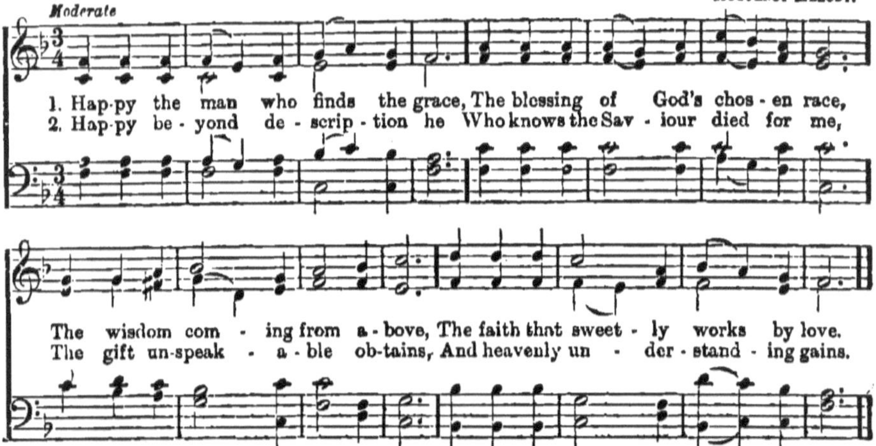

1. Happy the man who finds the grace, The blessing of God's chosen race,
The wisdom coming from above, The faith that sweetly works by love.

2. Happy beyond description he Who knows the Saviour died for me,
The gift unspeakable obtains, And heavenly understanding gains.

3 Wisdom divine! who tells the price
Of wisdom's costly merchandise?
Wisdom to silver we prefer,
And gold is dross compared to her.

4 Her hands are filled with length of days,
True riches, and immortal praise,
Riches of Christ on all bestowed,
And honour that descends from God.
—*C. Wesley.*

158 Jesus! and Shall it Ever Be. (ST. CRISPIN.—L.M.)

SIR G. J. ELVEY.

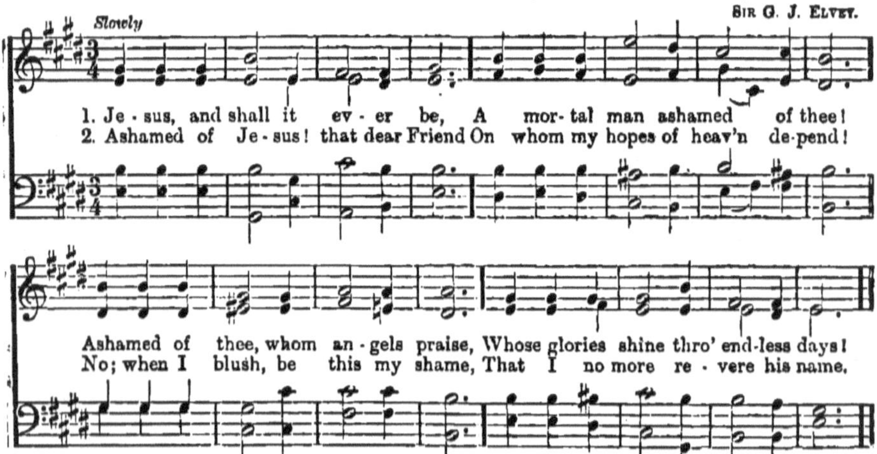

1. Jesus, and shall it ever be, A mortal man ashamed of thee!
Ashamed of thee, whom angels praise, Whose glories shine thro' endless days!

2. Ashamed of Jesus! that dear Friend On whom my hopes of heav'n depend!
No; when I blush, be this my shame, That I no more revere his name.

3 Ashamed of Jesus! yes, I may,
When I've no guilt to wash away;
No tear to wipe, no good to crave,
No fears to quell, no soul to save.

4 Till then—nor is my boasting vain—
Till then, I boast a Saviour slain!
And oh! may this my glory be,
That Christ is not ashamed of me!
—*J. Grigg.*

3 Down in the human heart,
  Crushed by the tempter,
  Feelings lie buried that grace can restore;
  Touched by a loving heart,
  Wakened by kindness,
  Chords that were broken will vibrate once more.

4 Rescue the perishing,
  Duty demands it;
  Strength for thy labour the Lord will provide;
  Back to the narrow way
  Patiently win them,
  Tell the poor wanderer a Saviour has died.

—*Fanny Crosby.*

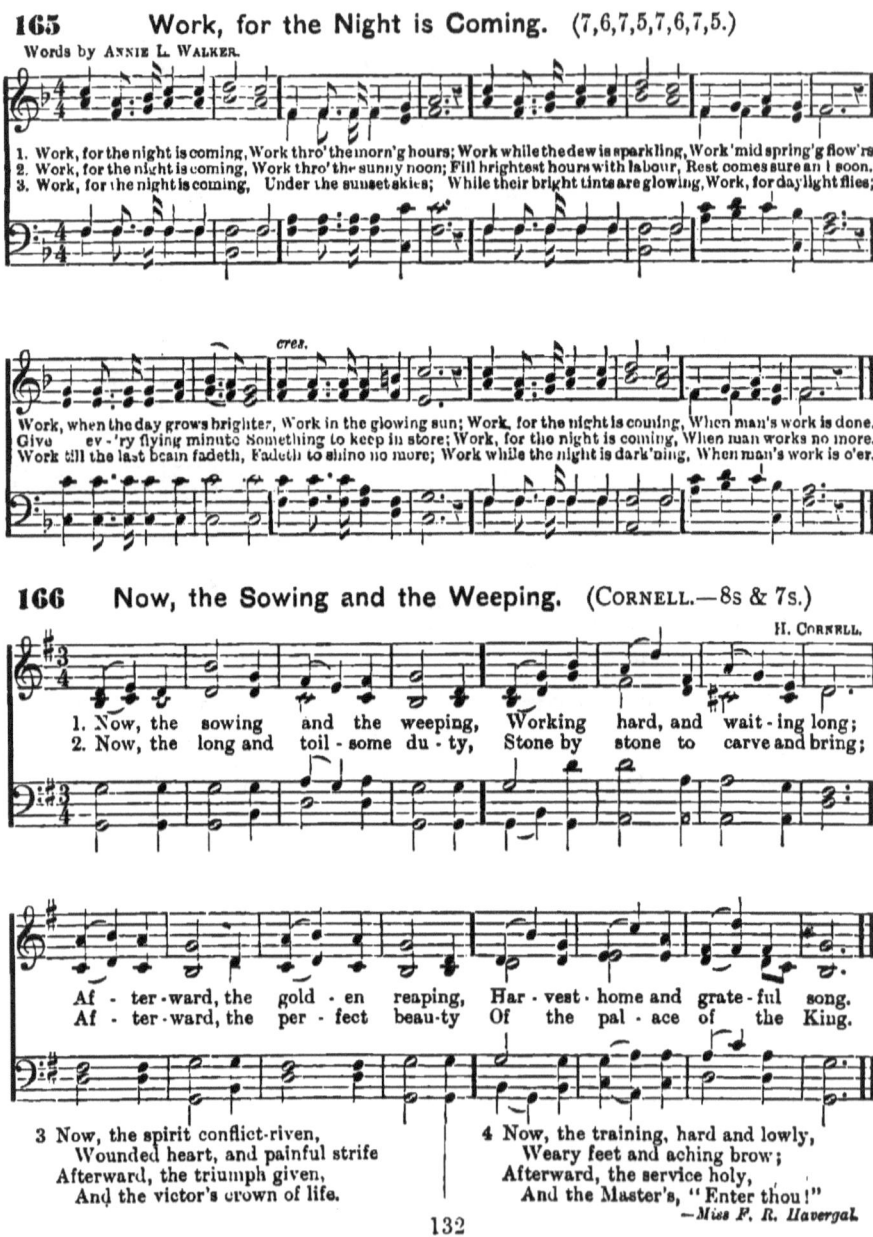

3 Now, the spirit conflict-riven,
  Wounded heart, and painful strife
Afterward, the triumph given,
  And the victor's crown of life.

4 Now, the training, hard and lowly,
  Weary feet and aching brow;
Afterward, the service holy,
  And the Master's, "Enter thou!"
                              —Miss F. R. Havergal.

191. Soldiers of the Cross, Arise! (CALEDONIA.—7,7,7,6.)

SCOTCH.

1. Soldiers of the cross, arise! Lo! your Leader from the skies
Waves before you glory's prize, The prize of victory.
Seize your armour, gird it on; Now the battle will be won;
See, the strife will soon be done; Then struggle manfully.

2. Now the fight of faith begin, Be no more the slaves of sin,
Strive the victor's palm to win, Trusting in the Lord:
Gird ye on the armour bright, Warriors of the King of light,
Never yield, nor lose by flight Your divine reward.

3 Jesus conquered when he fell,
Met and vanquished earth and hell;
Now he leads you on to swell
The triumphs of his cross.
Though all earth and hell appear,
Who will doubt, or who can fear?
God, our strength and shield, is near;
We cannot lose our cause.

4 Onward, then, ye hosts of God!
Jesus points the victor's rod;
Follow where your Leader trod;
You soon shall see his face.
Soon, your enemies all slain,
Crowns of glory you shall gain,
Soon you'll join that glorious train
Who shout their Saviour's praise.

—J. D. Watterbury.

195 Stand Up! Stand Up for Jesus! (WEBB.—7s & 6s.)
Words by G. DUFFIELD.

1. Stand up! stand up for Jesus! Ye soldiers of the cross!
Lift high his royal banner; It must not suffer loss:
*From vict'ry unto vict'ry His army will he lead,
Till ev'ry foe is vanquished, And Christ is Lord indeed.*

2. Stand up! stand up for Jesus! Stand in his strength alone;
The arm of flesh will fail you; Ye dare not trust your own:
*Put on the gospel armour, And, watching unto pray'r,
Where duty calls, or danger, Be never wanting there.*

3. Stand up! stand up for Jesus! The strife will not be long;
This day the noise of battle, The next the victor's song,
*To him that overcometh A crown of life shall be;
He with the King of glory Shall reign eternally.*

---

319 The Morning Light is Breaking. (7s & 6s—TUNE No. 195.)

1 The morning light is breaking;
　The darkness disappears;
The sons of earth are waking
　To penitential tears;
Each breeze that sweeps the ocean
　Brings tidings from afar,
Of nations in commotion
　Prepared for Zion's war.

2 See heathen nations bending
　Before the God we love,
And thousand hearts ascending
　In gratitude above;
While sinners, now confessing
　The gospel call obey,
And seek the Saviour's blessing,
　A nation in a day.

3 Blest river of salvation,
　Pursue thine onward way;
Flow thou to every nation,
　Nor in thy richness stay;
Stay not till all the lowly
　Triumphant reach their home;
Stay not till all the holy
　Proclaim, "The Lord is come!"
—S. F. Smith.

340. God Save Our Gracious Queen. (6,6,4,6,6,6,4.)

NATIONAL ANTHEM.

1. God save our gra-cious Queen, Long live our no-ble Queen,
   God save the Queen; Send her vic-to-ri-ous, Hap-py and glo-ri-ous,
   Long to reign o-ver us; God save the Queen.
2. Thro' ev-'ry chang-ing scene, O Lord, pre-serve our Queen;
   Long may she reign; Her heart in-spire and move With wisdom from a-bove;
   And in a na-tion's love Her throne main-tain.
3. Thy choic-est gifts in store On her be pleas'd to pour,
   Long may she reign; May she de-fend our laws, And ev-er give us cause
   To sing with heart and voice, God save the Queen.

299. America. (6, 4.—TUNE No. 340.)

1 My country ! 'tis of thee,
Sweet land of liberty,
Of thee I sing ;
Land where my fathers died !
Land of the pilgrims' pride !
From every mountain side
Let freedom ring !

2 My native country, thee,
Land of the noble, free,
Thy name I love ;
I love thy rocks and rills,
Thy woods and templed hills ;
My heart with rapture thrills
Like that above.

3 Let music swell the breeze,
And ring from all the trees
Sweet freedom's song ;
Let mortal tongues awake ;
Let all that breathe partake ;
Let rocks their silence break,
The sound prolong.

4 Our fathers' God ! to thee,
Author of liberty,
To thee we sing ;
Long may our land be bright
With freedom's holy light ;
Protect us by thy might,
Great God, our King !

—*Samuel F. Smith.*

359 God Be With You Till We Meet Again.

W. G. Tomer.

1. God be with you till we meet a-gain; By his counsels guide, uphold you,
   With his sheep se-cure-ly fold you; God be with you till we meet a-gain.
2. God be with you till we meet a-gain; 'Neath his wings se-cure-ly hide you,
   Dai-ly man-na still pro-vide you; God be with you till we meet a-gain.

CHORUS.

Till we meet, .. till we meet, Till we meet at Je-sus' feet;
Till we meet, till we meet again, Till we meet;
Till we meet, .. till we meet, God be with you till we meet a-gain.
Till we meet, till we meet a-gain.

3 God be with you till we meet again;
  When life's perils thick confound you,
  Put his arms unfailing round you;
  God be with you till we meet again.

4 God be with you till we meet again;
  Keep love's banner floating o'er you,
  Smite death's threatening wave before you;
  God be with you till we meet again.

J. E. Rankin.

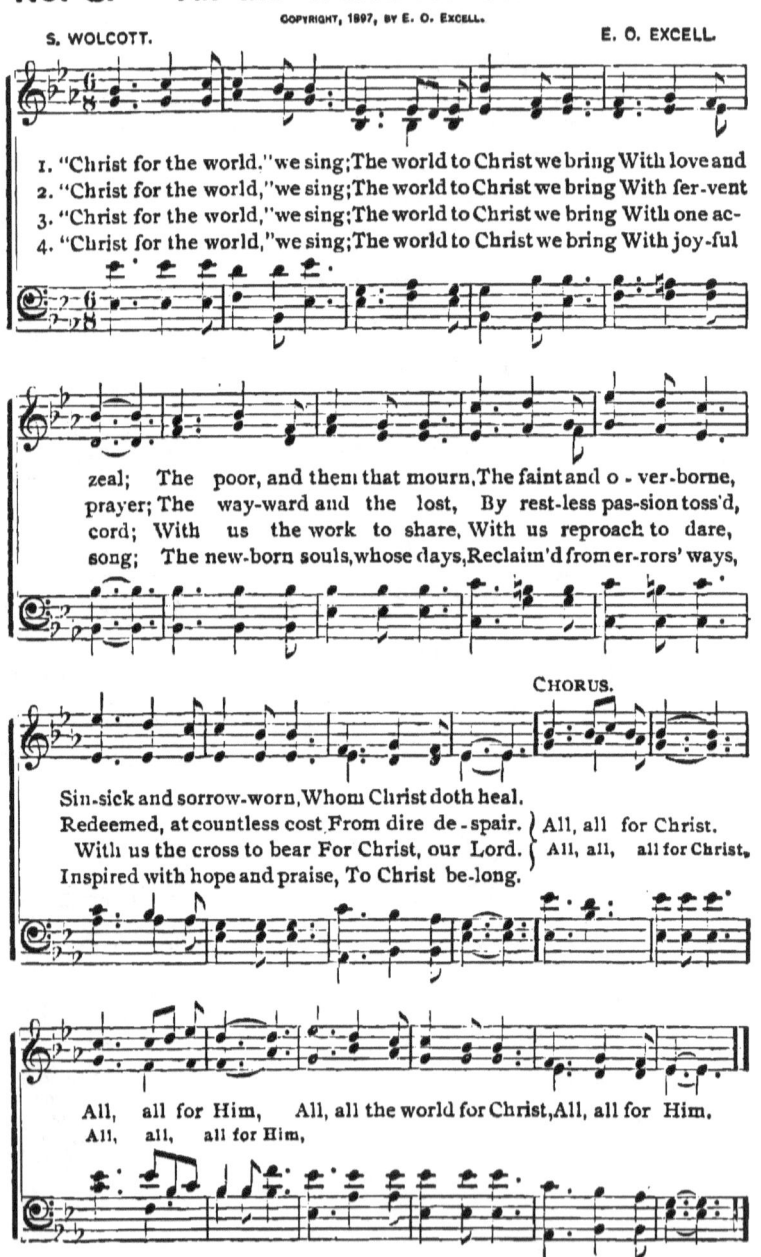

Improve the Golden Moments. Concluded.

Crowd them full of earnest la-bor, An-swer, "Here am I, send me."

No. 31. To the Front.

JOHN R. GOODWIN. COPYRIGHT, 1897, BY E. O. EXCELL. WORDS AND MUSIC. Partly written by Dr. S. B. JACKSON.

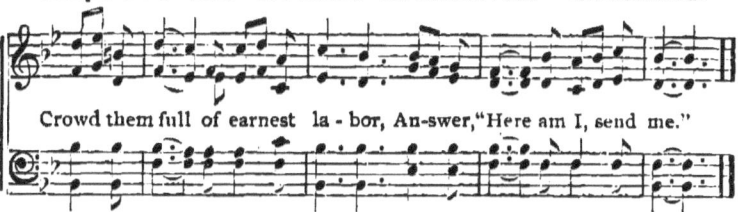

1. To the front! the war is rag-ing, Bold and fierce the hosts of sin;
2. In His name, and by His presence, We the hosts of sin de-fy;
3. To the front with ho-ly cour-age, Gird-ed with the armor bright;
4. Courage, sol-diers, in the arm-y Of our God! it is thro' thee

On the ranks of Christ are pressing, Firm in faith and strong to win.
Forward! lift the blood-stained banner; For the cross we dare and die.
Free sal-va-tion is our mot-to, We will con-quor in His might.
Sa-tan's pow-er must be broken, And his cap-tive ones set free.

CHORUS.

Press on-ward, Press on-ward With gos-pel armor shining bright;
on-ward, on-ward, on-ward, on-ward.

Press on-ward, Press on-ward! Be val-iant in the fight.
on-ward, on-ward, on-ward, on-ward.

On to Victory. Concluded.

On to vic-t'ry, On to vict'ry; All the world for Christ shall be our happy song.
marching on, marching on,

No. 49. Beautiful Isle.

JESSIE B. POUNDS. COPYRIGHT, 1897, BY E. O. EXCELL. WORDS AND MUSIC   J. S. FEARIS.

1. Somewhere the sun is shin-ing, Somewhere the song-birds dwell;
2. Somewhere the day is long-er, Somewhere the task is done;
3. Somewhere the load is lift-ed, Close by an o-pen gate;

Hush, then, thy sad re-pin-ing; God lives, and all is well.
Somewhere the heart is strong-er, Somewhere, the guer-don won.
Somewhere the clouds are rift-ed, Somewhere the an-gels wait!

CHORUS.

Some-where, Some-where, Beau-ti-ful Isle of Somewhere!
Some-where beauti-ful, beau-ti-ful Isle,

Land of the true where we live a-new,—Beauti-ful Isle of Somewhere!

Song of Triumph. Concluded.

No. 111. Closing Hymn.

JAMES EDMESTON.
COPYRIGHT, 1897, BY E. O. EXCELL.
E. O. EXCELL.

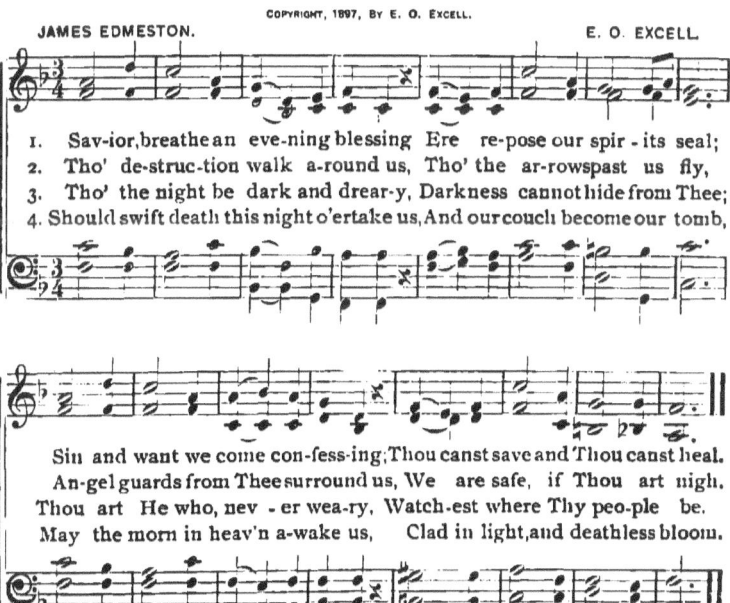

1. Sav-ior, breathe an eve-ning blessing Ere re-pose our spir-its seal;
2. Tho' de-struc-tion walk a-round us, Tho' the ar-rows past us fly,
3. Tho' the night be dark and drear-y, Darkness cannot hide from Thee;
4. Should swift death this night o'ertake us, And our couch become our tomb,

Sin and want we come con-fess-ing; Thou canst save and Thou canst heal.
An-gel guards from Thee surround us, We are safe, if Thou art nigh.
Thou art He who, nev - er wea-ry, Watch-est where Thy peo-ple be.
May the morn in heav'n a-wake us, Clad in light, and deathless bloom.

The
Methodist Book and Publishing House

INVITES a visit from every Delegate to the International Epworth League Convention

WE want the Delegates to make the Book-Room a favorite resort. Come in to rest if tired sight-seeing. Come in and take a look through the various departments of our house, the largest publishing house in Canada. If you want to write a letter, call in and you'll find pen, ink and paper at your service.

Some Special Souvenirs

Delegates will find in our store a choice stock of Souvenirs. Among them

SOUVENIR VIEWS OF TORONTO. Comprising Photo-Engravings of Public Buildings, Churches, Residences, Street Scenes and Glimpses of Scenery. Price .... .10

GLASS PAPER WEIGHTS, with Views of Public Buildings....... .25

DIAMOND JUBILEE SUNDAY-SCHOOL SOUVENIR CARDS. Each 4 cts.; per dozen.. .40

SOUVENIR SPOONS, BADGES, ETC., ETC.

CANADIAN BOOKS

No doubt many of our American visitors will like to carry back with them books descriptive of Canadian life or history, works of the Canadian poets, etc. Of these we have ample supply, and would recommend the works of such authors as WITHROW, McDOUGALL, MACLEAN, E. R. YOUNG, THOMSON, ROBERTS, RAND, CAMPBELL, SCOTT, and others. Space forbids mention of the books, but these will be shown at our counters.

CHEAP EDITIONS OF
AMERICAN AUTHORS

We have a large supply of English editions of books by popular American authors, very much cheaper than the American copyright editions. Have a look through these.

EPWORTH LEAGUE SUPPLIES

The Delegates will no doubt be interested in looking through our range of Epworth League requisites and literature. **Crews' "Epworth League Manual"** and **Bartlett's "Junior League Hand-Book"** may well be taken by every delegate. They both are packed with useful hints.

Be sure to give us a call.

WILLIAM BRIGGS,
Methodist Book and Publishing House,
29-33 Richmond Street West, - - TORONTO, ONT.

MASSEY-HARRIS
..WHEEL..

NO Castings or Stampings are used in its construction. All the joints are made from Solid Steel Forgings. The Tubing used is the Mannesman Seamless Tubing. English Perry Chains. Christy Saddles. Enamel, Black and Maroon Finish.

MASSEY-HARRIS CO., LTD.

Local Salesrooms: Factory:
Cor. Yonge and Adelaide Sts.   927 KING ST. WEST,
and 1388 Queen St. West   TORONTO, CAN.

In Toronto

the headquarters for tourists and transient visitors is

Webb's Restaurant

situated right in the heart of the city, at 66 and 68 Yonge St. In size and equipment it well deserves the name of the Largest and Most Complete Restaurant in Canada. The front elevator runs to the Ladies' Dining Room, with comfortable waiting and retiring rooms adjoining. Parcels are checked for the day free of charge.

THE **Harry Webb Co.** LTD.

RESTAURANT:
66 AND 68 YONGE STREET.

CATERING ESTABLISHMENT:
447 YONGE STREET.

Canada's Greatest Store.

REPRESENTING A VILLAGE OF BUSY PEOPLE, ALL UNDER ONE ROOF, WITH

- —Over Seven Acres of Floor-Space.
- —Nearly eighteen hundred Employees.
- —A Manufacturing Department with 339 sewing machines, run by electric power, turning out 2,400 complete garments every day, all of which are sold in our own store.
- —Half-a-hundred Different Stocks.
- —A Delivery Department consisting of 76 horses and 45 waggons.
- —The Largest Private Electric Plant in Canada, having 3 dynamos with a capacity of 2,250 incandescent lights, and 200 arc lights.

DELEGATES to the Epworth League Convention will be interested in knowing that this is the largest store in all Canada. It sells everything that goes well together, including Dry Goods, House Furnishings, Sporting Goods, Books and Stationery, Clothing and Shoes, Drugs and Medicines, Groceries, etc. This store is to Toronto what Wanamaker is to Philadelphia, Macey to New York, Jordan Marsh to Boston and Marshall Field to Chicago. The comfort and convenience of shoppers has been considered to a remarkable degree, with places to sit and rest, read and write, eat and drink, meet friends and check parcels.

Delegates are cordially invited to visit the store. It is at your service whoever you are. Make yourself at home; come here to meet your friends, check your parcels or write your letters. No need to spend a cent unless you wish to. We want to know you and have you know us.

THE T. EATON CO. LIMITED

190 to 200 YONGE STREET,
10 to 18 QUEEN STREET WEST,
11 to 29 JAMES STREET,
15 to 19 ALBERT STREET,
All under One Roof.

Main Entrance—
190 YONGE ST.,
TORONTO, ONT.

... OFFICIAL ...

E. L. Jewelers

Stands: ARMOURIES and MASSEY HALL

Store: 156 YONGE ST.   Factory: 5 & 7 RICHMOND ST. W.

We manufacture and sell at Right Prices

Silver E. L. Pins
Silver Enamelled E. L. Pins
Gold Enamelled E. L. Pins
Silver E. L. Bangle Pins
Gilt E. L. Souvenir Badge
Silver E. L. Ladies' Ribbon Guards, etc., etc.

Our Specialty

DIAMONDS
WATCHES
JEWELRY
SILVERWARE
NOVELTIES
CLOCKS
OPTICAL GOODS
ETC., ETC.

INVITE INSPECTION

Ambrose Kent & Sons
GOLD AND SILVERSMITHS
156 Yonge St. - TORONTO

..CANADA'S..
Leading Retail Store

SEVEN MAGNIFICENT STORIES

South-West corner Yonge and Queen Sts.
TORONTO'S BUSIEST CORNER

THE great stores of a large city always command the interest of visitors. While Toronto has many fine stores, that of the **ROBERT SIMPSON CO., Limited**, stands out exceptional, and is without comparison in Canada. It is a splendid specimen of modern architecture; its structural metal work, fire-proofed in terra cotta, making it an absolutely fire-proof building. With high ceilings and broad aisles, it is one of the most comfortable stores in the hottest summer days. Symmetry, system and science mark its construction from basement to dome, from north to south, from east to west.

There is hardly anything the shopper will want that cannot be found within its walls. Primarily and essentially a great dry goods store, the finest in Dress Goods, Silks, Trimmings, Mantles, Millinery, Gloves and Smallwares, Men's and Boys' Clothing are on sale in its several departments.

Outside of these and many other staple lines, the store-planning includes a thoroughly equipped drug store, under the management of graduated pharmacists; one of the best grocery stores in the city, and a basement, unique in construction, where Household Goods and Novelties of all kinds will be found.

The management are always glad to have those who come as strangers to the city make themselves at home within the store, and wander through its many acres of floor-space at their own sweet will and pleasure.

(ASSESSMENT SYSTEM)

HEAD OFFICE:

Cor. Richmond and Bay Streets, TORONTO, CAN.

OFFICE FOR GREAT BRITAIN—24 Charing Cross, London, Eng.
OFFICE FOR IRELAND—5 Royal Avenue, Belfast, Ireland.
OFFICE FOR UNITED STATES—6340 Monroe Avenue, Chicago, Ill.

OFFICERS OF SUPREME COURT:

ORONHYATEKHA, M.D., S.C.R., Toronto, Canada.
EDWARD BOTTERELL, P.S.C.R., House of Commons, Ottawa, Can.
HON. D. D. AITKIN, M.C., S.V.C.R., Flint, Mich., U.S.
JOHN A. McGILLIVRAY, Q.C., S.S., Toronto, Canada.
H. A. COLLINS, S.T., Toronto, Canada.
THOMAS MILLMAN, M.D., M.R.C.S.Eng., S. Physician, Toronto.
HON. JUDGE W. WEDDERBURN, S.C., Hampton, N.B.

BENEFITS GIVEN BY THE I.O.F.

In addition to the social and fraternal privileges which a Forester enjoys by virtue of his membership in this great fraternal Order, he secures the following substantial benefits:

For himself during his lifetime:

A.—Furnished by the Subordinate Courts.

1. —Free medical attendance of the Court Physician within whose jurisdiction the brother is taken sick. Some Courts, in addition, furnish medicine free, as well as trained nurses, if deemed necessary by the Court.

B.—Furnished by the Supreme Court.

2. —A Sick Benefit of $3.00 a week for the first two weeks, and $5.00 a week for the next ten weeks, and as provided in Section 224 (5) of the Order, $3.00 a week for an additional twelve weeks.
3. —A Total and Permanent Disability Benefit of $250, $500, $1,000, $1,500, $2,000, or $2,500.

For his beneficiaries at his death:
4. —A Funeral Benefit of $50.
5. A Mortuary Benefit of $500, $1,000, $2,000, $3,000, $4,000, or $5,000.

Cost to join the Order is only $6.50 to $12.00, according to Amount of Benefit Taken.

SAFEGUARD FOR MEMBERS.

The following most important legislative provision relative to the liabilities of the members was also secured in the last Act:

10. The liabilities of any member of the Society shall be limited to the assessments, dues, fees, capitation tax and fines of which, at the date at which he ceases to be a member by withdrawal, expulsion, suspension, or non-payment of assessments or dues or otherwise, notice has been actually given by the Society, or which under its constitutions and laws have matured and become due; Provided that no member, or his beneficiary, shall be entitled to any pecuniary benefit of the Society during the time such member is in default with respect to the payment of any assessments, dues, fees, capitation tax or fines; and the provisions of this section shall be printed on each and every policy issued by the Society.

THE I.O.F. UNDER GOVERNMENT INSPECTION.

The Supreme Court makes annual returns to the Board of Trade of Great Britain and Ireland and to various Insurance Departments in Canada and the United States. The Order is subject to and has frequently received the inspection of a number of Insurance Departments.

THE I.O.F. INVESTMENTS.

The Supreme Court, under the amendments to its Act of Incorporation secured from the Parliament of Canada in 1896, maintains a Government deposit of $100,000 dollars in Canada, also of £20,000 sterling in Great Britain and Ireland, and a deposit of $50,000 in the United States, the balance being deposited with sound monetary institutions or invested in first mortgages upon improved real estate and in municipal securities. The following table shows where some of the funds are thus deposited:

Deposit Insurance Department, Canada		$100,000 00
" " "	Great Britain	97,333 33
" " "	United States	50,000 00
Loan to New Brunswick Government		20,000 00
First Mortgages on Real Estate		1,166,320 02
Real Estate (Temple Building)		263,600 00
Municipal and School Debentures		92,553 10
Various Bank Deposits		168,988 17

Total Surplus 31st May, 1897, $2,233,326.89

The unexampled prosperity and growth of the I.O.F. are due to the fact that its foundations have been laid on a SOLID FINANCIAL BASIS, and every department of the Order has been managed on business principles, thereby securing for all Foresters large and varied benefits at the lowest possible cost consistent with SAFETY and PERMANENCE.

I.O.F. RESULTS SUMMARIZED.

THE MAGNIFICENT BENEFITS PAID.

Benefits paid last *Year* (1896).........	$ 820,941 91
Benefits paid last *Five Years*	2,754,039 14
Benefits paid last *Ten Years*	3,462,142 79
Benefits paid since organization (to 31st May, 1897).......................	4,563,742 21

THE GROWTH OF THE MEMBERSHIP.

Membership 1st July, 1881....	367	Date of Reorganization.	
Membership 31st Dec., 1881...	1,019	Increase in *Six Months*.........	652
Membership 31st Dec., 1886...	5,804	Increase in *First Five Years* ...	4,785
Membership 31st Dec., 1891...	32,303	Increase in *Second Five Years*..	26,499
Membership 31st Dec., 1896...	102,838	Increase in *Third Five Years*...	70,535

THE INCREASES LAST YEAR (1896).

Increase of *Benefits Paid*..............	$ 135,941 73
Increase of *Assessment Income*	228,932 00
Increase of *Total Income*	347,901 19
Increase of *Net Assets*	438,114 34
Increase of *Surplus Funds*	455,110 92
Increase of *Assurance in Force*........	20,763,500 00

THE EXPANSION OF THE SURPLUS.

Surplus 1st July, 1881..	$	Date of Reorganization.	
Surplus 31st Dec., 1881.	4,568 55	Increase in *Six Months*..	$ 4,568 55
Surplus 31st Dec., 1886.	53,981 28	Increase in *1st Five Years*	49,412 73
Surplus 31st Dec., 1891.	408,798 20	Increase in *2nd Five Years*	354,816 92
Surplus 31st Dec., 1896.	2,015,484 38	Increase in *3rd Five Years*	1,606,686 18

THE MEMBERS AND THEIR ASSURANCE (at 31st December, 1896).

Year.	Total Membership.	Insurance Carried.	Total Surplus.	Surplus per Capita.	Death Rate per 1,000.
1881	1,019	$ 1,140,000	$ 4,568 55	$ 4 48	4.50
1882	1,134	1,276,000	2,967 93	2 61	11.00
1883	2,210	2,490,000	10,857 65	4 91	4.73
1884	2,558	2,923,000	23,081 85	9 01	4.23
1885	3,642	4,283,000	29,802 42	8 18	7.76
1886	5,804	6,764,000	53,981 28	9 30	4.85
1887	7,811	9,120,000	81,384 41	10 44	5.78
1888	11,800	13,714,000	117,821 96	9 98	6.43
1889	17,349	20,078,000	188,130 36	10 84	5.85
1890	24,604	28,498,000	283,967 20	11 54	5.18
1891	32,303	39,395,000	408,798 20	12 65	6.40
1892	43,024	53,243,000	580,597 85	13 49	6.25
1893	54,484	67,781,000	858,857 89	15 76	5.47
1894	70,055	86,506,500	1,187,225 11	16 94	5.47
1895	86,521	108,027,500	1,560,373 46	18 03	5.67
1896	102,838	128,791,000	2,015,484 38	19 60	5.50

The I.O.F. is doing business in the Dominion of Canada, in the United States, and in Great Britain and Ireland.

"TEMPLE BUILDING."

THE ILLUSTRATION on the opposite page represents the magnificent Temple at the corner of Richmond and Bay Streets, Toronto, the home of the INDEPENDENT ORDER OF FORESTERS. The building, which is one of the "objects of interest" that every visitor to Toronto should see, has been erected under the special superintendence of Dr. Oronhyatekha, Supreme Chief Ranger of the Order, and will be, if not the best, certainly among the best and most complete of its kind in the Dominion. The erection of this handsome edifice was commenced in the spring of 1895, the corner-stone being laid by His Excellency the Earl of Aberdeen, Governor-General of Canada, on the 30th of May in that year.

The first two stories are built of Credit Valley brown stone, and the remaining eight stories of brownish red brick, trimmed throughout with Credit Valley and Connecticut brown stone. The whole structure is lined with, and the steel therein is protected by, fire-proof porous terra cotta of superior manufacture. As a matter of fact, the whole building will be as thoroughly fire-proof as modern science can make it, there being nothing to burn except the window-frames and sashes.

The building will contain two thoroughly fire-proof elevator shafts, in which will be three of the largest and finest elevators in the city, besides the stairs, which will be of steel, slate and marble.

The roof also, will be of absolutely fire-proof material, on which bonfires might be built without injury to it or the building.

There are four tiers of fire-proof vaults in the building, extending from the basement to the ninth story. To guard against any possible danger of fire, within or without, two standing water pipes have been placed in the building with steam pump to make pressure and hose connections on every floor.

The Temple will be heated by steam and lighted by electricity produced on the premises by the latest and most approved machinery. Ventilation has received special attention, and the sanitary arrangements are in every way up to date.

The Temple is intended as an office building, but a portion of it will be devoted to other purposes. A bank will occupy part of the main floor, while near it will be another large monetary institution, and a publishing house will occupy rooms on three floors. In the fourth and fifth stories of the western section will be magnificent Court Rooms and necessary adjuncts for Forestric and other society meetings. A magnificent assembly room will be immediately above these, occupying the sixth and seventh stories. The eighth story will be wholly occupied by the Supreme Court offices and staff. The ninth and tenth stories will be handsomely fitted up for the use of the Masonic fraternity, by which they will be occupied.

The Temple has been erected under the professional supervision of Mr. George W. Gouinlock, who has certainly succeeded in producing an excellently planned and ornate building, and so well proportioned that few would realize when looking at it that it is the highest building yet erected in Canada. As a matter of fact, it is 140 feet high, exclusive of the tower, which adds 45 feet, making a total height of 185 feet from sidewalk to the top of the tower. From the roof of this eminence an extensive view may be enjoyed of the city and surrounding country, and even Niagara Falls may be seen. The observation tower will be open to the public.

The building is most conveniently located, being only half a block from the new City Hall, less than 200 feet from the City Registry Office, a block distant from Osgoode Hall, and the same distance from several lines of electric cars.

"Temple Building"

CORNER RICHMOND AND BAY STS.,

✤ ✤ TORONTO ✤ ✤

A Thoroughly Fireproof Structure. · *Highest Business Block in Canada.*

HEADQUARTERS OF

The Independent Order of Foresters

THE BEST FRATERNAL SOCIETY IN THE WORLD.

Delegates are requested as far as possible to patronize our Advertisers, as they have helped us with our Convention expenses.

Bicycles for Delegates

HIGH-GRADE wheels for RENT during the Convention at convention prices. You can see more of our beautiful City by RENTING A BICYCLE than by any other means of conveyance . . . . . .

THE RICHARD SIMPSON CO., Limited,
(Near Massey Hall and the Armouries)

242 Yonge Street, Corner Louisa Street

320 Queen St. E.   472 Queen St. W.   784 Queen St. E.

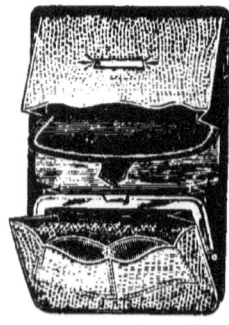

HEADQUARTERS FOR

**Account Books   Stationery   Bookbinding
Office Supplies   Paper   Leather Goods
Typewriter Supplies**

AGENTS FOR

Wirt Fountain Pen   Caligraph Typewriter
Edison Mimeograph

THE **BROWN BROS.**, LIMITED
Complete Stationery House

64-68 King Street East, - - TORONTO

GRIMSBY PARK The Great Canadian Summer Resort, situated on the south shore of Lake Ontario, midway between Niagara Falls and Hamilton. Splendid Beach, Boating, Bathing, Fishing. One hundred acres of Forest and Green Sward. Beautiful Walks and Avenues. Two Hotels—Lake View House and Park House. Terms: **$1.00 to $2.00** per day. Over 200 Cottages in the Park. The best talent on the Continent secured for Sermons, Lectures, Recitals, Concerts, Vocal and Instrumental Entertainments. Callsthenic and Physical Culture Classes. "The Park Temple," the most unique structure in America, will hold about 6,000 people. Park brilliantly illuminated by electricity. Excellent Steamboat Service from Toronto. Grand Trunk Station on the grounds. Illustrated Programmes giving all particulars may be had at the Methodist Book Room, Toronto, or sent post free on application to Mr. B. C. FAIRFIELD, St. Catharines. Delegates to the Epworth League Convention will find the Park the most delightful Summer Resort in Ontario.

NOAH PHELPS,   **W. C. WILKINSON,**
PRESIDENT.   SECRETARY, TORONTO.

...PUT THIS DOWN...

Visitors can Make Expenses by ordering a handsome SUIT or OVERCOAT from   **S. CORRIGAN**

113 YONGE STREET . . . . .   **The Leading Tailor** ● ● ● ●

ESTABLISHED 1874

Imported Suitings from **$15.00** up.   Imported Pantings from **$3.50** up.
Imported Overcoatings from **$14.00** up.

CALL EARLY AND INSPECT STOCK AND PRICES.

Canadian Summer Resort Guide

Price 25c. mailed.

A beautifully illustrated, handsomely bound book, describing many of the charming **Summer Scenes in Canada,** containing concise and accurate information as to **Excursion Rates, Tourist Routes and Views, with Maps of the Unrivalled Fishing, Hunting and Summer Resorts of Canada.** Epworth League Delegates should not miss the opportunity for visiting some of the many **Beautiful Resorts adjacent to Toronto,** easily accessible by boat or rail. No more suitable souvenir can be obtained for your friends at home or abroad.

Copies of "Canadian Summer Resort Guide" for sale at
CONVENTION HEADQUARTERS,
Newsdealers, or
Office of Publication :
Room 45, No. 34 Victoria Street, Toronto.

Good Tailoring

VISITORS to Toronto are reminded that this city is noted for the superiority of its MERCHANT TAILORS' work. There are no better dressed men anywhere than the residents of this prosperous place. We hold a first place among the best houses of the city, and if needing clothing you will find it advantageous to see our stock before ordering. We carry large lines of all that is best for your selection, both for style and durability, and no firm can give you better value for the money expended. Our prices are always the lowest consistent with good workmanship.

A really durable well-made suit can be got here for **EIGHTEEN DOLLARS,** and "Ideal Trousers" at **FIVE DOLLARS** are good trousers. Perhaps you do not want any clothing now, but call and see us anyway, leave your measure with us, and samples can be sent when you do.

JOS. J. FOLLETT,
Good Tailoring   -   -   181 Yonge Street.

TORONTO'S LARGEST

Retail Grocers

Headquarters for . . .

CAMPERS' and PICNIC SUPPLIES

Cooked TONGUES and HAMS

. . . PASTRY . . .

BISCUITS and CRACKERS

. . MACAROONS . .

MacWillie Bros.  Phones, 309, 326

GROCERS

Confederation Life Building, TORONTO.

*Free Delivery, all Trains and Steamboats,
Lorne Park, Long Branch, etc., etc.*

The Queens Hotel, TORONTO

IS one of the largest in Canada, and is the headquarters of members of the Royal Family, Governors-General, Prime Ministers and all distinguished English and American visitors when in Toronto ✤ ✤ ✤ ✤ ✤ ✤

Terms: $3.00 to $5.00
ACCORDING TO LOCATION

McGAW & WINNETT, - - PROPRIETORS

Illustrating a line of work properly taught in the ...

Central Business College,
TORONTO

Special departments for

Commercial Branches, Shorthand and Typewriting.

Present Session continues to July 30.

Teachers appointed as Delegates to Epworth League Convention can arrange to spend July at College, less two days.

GET PARTICULARS

Address—

W. H. SHAW, Principal.

Chautauqua
The Original Assembly
On the way to or from .... **TORONTO**

You may never have a better chance to visit this world-famed institution. "NOT A DULL DAY ALL SUMMER." You will find something interesting and inspiring every day from June 29th to Aug. 24th.

EPWORTH LEAGUERS will receive a warm welcome from the Chautauqua Epworth League in the commodious Methodist Episcopal Headquarters. You will not be a stranger in a strange land. C. L. S. C. MEMBERS may depend upon a cordial greeting at the Chautauqua Office, and in the Grove.

Beautiful Natural Scenery   **Recreation of every Legitimate Kind**
Famous Speakers and Readers   **Daily Religious Gatherings**

Bishop McCabe, Miss Willard, Dr. Buckley, Dr. Kelley, Pres. Crawford, Bishop Vincent, Mrs. Maud Booth, and scores beside.

COST OF LIVING AT THE LOWEST. Toronto Tickets good for stop-over.

For full information, address, **W. A. DUNCAN, Sec., Box 63, Chautauqua, N.Y.**

A. E. Ames & Co.   Bankers and Brokers

NEW YORK and CHICAGO DRAFTS bought and sold.

STOCKS and BONDS dealt in on all principal Exchanges on commission.

MONEY TO LEND on marketable stocks.

DEPOSITS RECEIVED at 4 per cent. interest, subject to repayment on demand.

10 King Street West,   -   -   **TORONTO, ONT.**

Shall the Visiting Members of the Epworth League go Hungry?

Not if we can help it.

Special arrangements and an attractive Bill of Fare to help meet the requirements of 20,000 strangers.

Daily capacity, 3,000 meals.

St. Lawrence Coffee House, Lunch and Dining Rooms, 78-80 King St. East.

Shaftesbury Coffee House, Lunch and Dining Rooms, 23 Queen St. West.

Both places in the neighborhood of Massey Hall and the Metropolitan Church.

ESTABLISHED 1831.

 ## Yonge St. Wharf

**PROPRIETORS: MESSRS. W. & R. FREELAND.
LESSEES: MESSRS. D. MILLOY & CO.**

THIS wharf is the principal steamboat landing in the city. The passenger steamers from all points on the lake land and embark their passengers here. It is also the central receiving and distributing point for an immense fruit business by boat and rail. A special railway siding has been put in to handle this traffic expeditiously. The following is a list of the steamers making daily trips, viz.:

The magnificent steel steamer *Chippewa* (licensed to carry 2,000 passengers), *Corona* (1,500 passengers), and *Chicora* (872 passengers), of the Niagara River Line, for **Niagara-on-the-Lake** (32 miles), **Queenston** (40 miles), **Lewiston** (40 miles), and the **Falls**, at 7 and 11 a.m., 2 and 4.45 p.m. The staunch steamer *Lakeside* (540 passengers), for **Port Dalhousie** (32 miles) and **St. Catharines** (36 miles), at 3.40 p.m.; the splendid iron steamers of the Richelieu & Ontario Navigation Co.'s Line (400 passengers) for the **Thousand Islands, Montreal, Quebec** and the **Saguenay**, at 2 p.m.; the steamer *Greyhound* (480 passengers), for **Lorne Park** (15 miles), at 9.30 a.m., 2 and 5 p.m., and **Oakville** (21 miles), 9.30 a.m., 2 and 5 and 9 p.m.

The **Verral Baggage Transfer Co.** have an office here, and will attend to the delivery of trunks and all other baggage in any part of the city, and operate the Omnibus line to all the hotels.

SPECIAL EXCURSION
..TO..

Niagara Falls

For the Delegates attending the Convention and their friends has been arranged by the Executive for . . . .

Monday, July 19th

By the Palatial Steamers of the NIAGARA RIVER LINE . . . .

Leaving Toronto, foot of Yonge Street, at 7 a.m., 9 a.m. and 11 a.m.

And returning again at night, giving several hours to view the beauties of the **Niagara River** and the vicinity of the wonderful **Falls**.

The Number of Excursionists will be limited to One Thousand

TICKETS will be on sale at Headquarters at the low rate of **$1.25 each.**

DO NOT FAIL TO VISIT NIAGARA, ONE OF THE GREATEST SIGHTS IN AMERICA

Do not fail to see the great Cyclorama, "JERUSALEM AT THE TIME OF THE CRUCIFIXION," Front St., adjoining the Union Depot. Tickets 25 cents, to be procured at Headquarters Building (the Armoury).

WESTERN ASSURANCE COMPANY.

Head Office, Corner Wellington and Scott Streets, Toronto

A. M. SMITH, President.   GEORGE A. COX, Vice-President.

Capital Subscribed,	$2,000,000
Capital Paid up,	1,000,000
Annual Income, over	2,150,000

Agencies in Principal Cities and Towns in Canada and United States.

Niagara River Line

THE SHORT AND PICTURESQUE WATER ROUTE BETWEEN.....

TORONTO, NIAGARA FALLS and BUFFALO

...STEEL STEAMERS...
CHICORA ~ CORONA ~ CHIPPEWA

LEAVING LEWISTON, QUEENSTON, NIAGARA and TORONTO four times daily (except Sunday). Connections with New York Central and Michigan Central Railways, and Gorge Electric and Canadian Electric Roads. The only route giving views of Falls, Rapids, Brock's Monument and all the beautiful scenery of the lower Niagara River . .

TOURISTS CAN LEAVE TORONTO IN MORNING, HAVE SIX HOURS AT FALLS, AND BE BACK FOR DINNER IN EVENING.

Tickets at all principal Offices ◊ JOHN FOY
... MANAGER.

BX
8205
A54
1897

3rd International
Convention of the
Epworth League

PLEASE DO NOT REMOVE
CARDS OR SLIPS FROM THIS POCKET

UNIVERSITY OF TORONTO LIBRARY

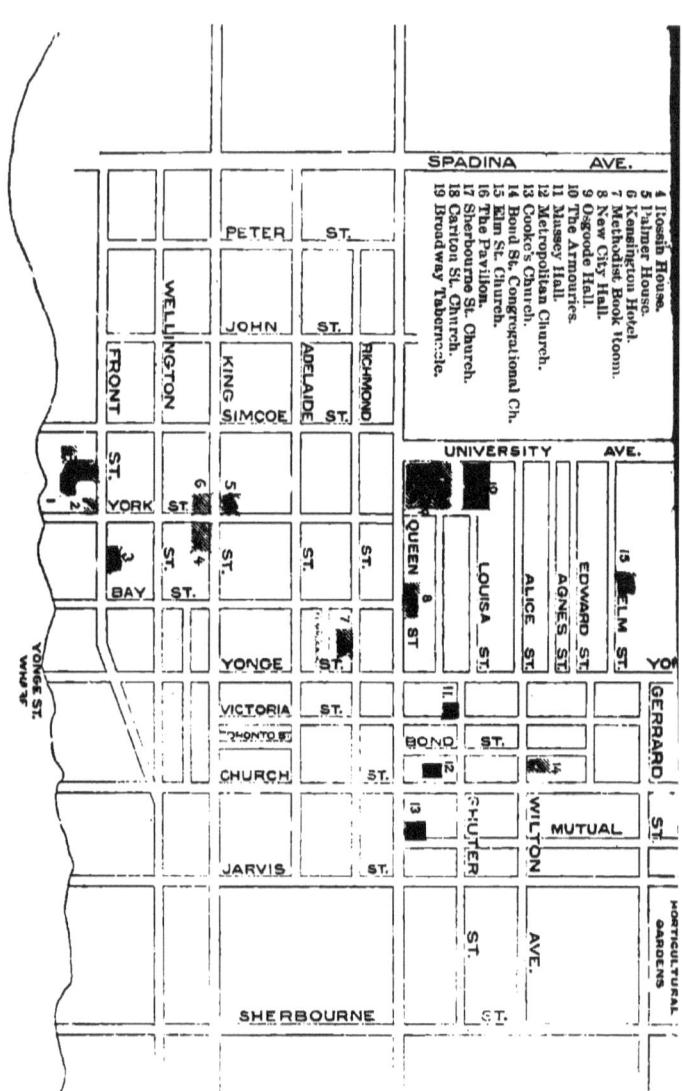

www.ingramcontent.com/pod-product-compliance
Lightning Source LLC
Chambersburg PA
CBHW030250170426
43202CB00009B/688